LEADING THE WAY THROUGH EPHESIANS

LEADING THE WAY THROUGH

EPHESIANS

MICHAEL YOUSSEF

HARVEST HOUSE PUBLISHERS
EUGENE, OREGON

Cover design by Harvest House Publishers, Inc., Eugene, Oregon

Cover photo © iStockphoto.com/erhandayi, BrianAJackson

Published in association with the literary agency of Wolgemuth & Associates. Inc.

Leading the Way Through Ephesians
Copyright © 2012 by Michael Youssef
Published by Harvest House Publishers
Eugene, Oregon 97402
www.harvesthousepublishers.com

Library of Congress Cataloging-in-Publication Data

Youssef, Michael.
Leading the way through Ephesians / Michael Youssef.
p. cm.
Includes bibliographical references.
ISBN 978-0-7369-5162-3 (pbk.)
ISBN 978-0-7369-5163-0 (eBook)
1. Bible. N.T. Ephesians—Commentaries. I. Title.
BS2695.53.Y68 2012
227'.507—dc23

2012015995

Printed in the United States of America

12 13 14 15 16 17 18 19 20 / VP-NI / 10 9 8 7 6 5 4 3 2 1

To all faithful preachers, teachers, and Christian leaders
who seek to accurately expound the Word of God
from pulpits or in Sunday school classes or in home Bible study groups.

Acknowledgments

First, I offer all my thanksgiving to the Father in heaven whose Holy Spirit has laid on my heart the writing of this series for the glory of Jesus. I am also immensely grateful to the Lord for sending me an able and gifted editor and compiler of my material in Jim Denney.

Special thanks to the entire team at Harvest House Publishers—and especially to Bob Hawkins Jr., LaRae Weikert, and Rod Morris, who shared my vision and made this dream a reality.

My expression of thanks would not be complete without mentioning the patience and perseverance of Robert and Andrew Wolgemuth of Wolgemuth and Associates, Inc. literary agency for managing the many details of such an undertaking.

My earnest prayer is that, as I leave this legacy to the next generation, God would raise up great men and women to faithfully serve their generation by accurately interpreting the Word of God.

Contents

Introduction

Ephesians 1:1-2

When I was growing up in Egypt, we lived next door to a wealthy eccentric who owned a great deal of real estate. In spite of his vast wealth, he lived like the poorest of the poor. He could have easily afforded a private doctor, yet when he or his wife needed medical attention, they would stand in line for hours at the government-run health clinic. Instead of enjoying fine dining at elegant restaurants, he and his wife bought the cheapest food and often went without meals in order to scrimp and save.

Here was a man who lived in poverty even though he possessed great wealth. After he died, the people who settled his estate found large cans of money that he had hidden throughout his house. It was money he never used or enjoyed, money that did him no good whatsoever.

We shake our heads in amazement and wonder, *How can a man of such wealth choose to live like a pauper?* Yet I find that many Christians have a lot in common with this man. Many of us truly live in spiritual poverty, even to the point of spiritual malnutrition, while we have at our fingertips an infinite supply of spiritual riches.

In Ephesians, the apostle Paul reveals to us the spiritual blessings we have in Christ Jesus. Through the years, this letter has been described as:

- the believer's bank
- the Christian's checkbook and
- the treasure house of the Bible

Ephesians explains how, by means of the death and resurrection of Jesus Christ, we have access to the limitless riches and power of the Holy Spirit. Ephesians is as foundational to an understanding of the New Testament as the book of Joshua is to the Old Testament.

The heavenly places

The letter we call "Ephesians" was probably not written specifically or solely to the Christians in the city of Ephesus. The commonly accepted text of Ephesians begins with this greeting:

> Paul, an apostle of Christ Jesus by the will of God,
>
> To the saints who are in Ephesus, and are faithful in Christ Jesus:
>
> Grace to you and peace from God our Father and the Lord Jesus Christ (Ephesians 1:1-2).

The best and earliest Greek manuscripts of Ephesians, however, do not contain the phrase "who are in Ephesus." The best manuscripts read simply, "To the saints, the faithful in Christ Jesus." This suggests that the phrase "who are in Ephesus" was not written by Paul, but was added later. The Book of Acts tells us that Paul of Tarsus spent a great deal of time in the church at Ephesus, yet this letter makes no reference to people Paul knew in Ephesus or his experiences among them. Instead, Paul seems to know the readers of this letter by reputation, not personal acquaintance, because he writes in 1:15, "because I have heard of your faith in the Lord Jesus and your love toward all the saints..."

The Ephesian believers were certainly *among* Paul's intended recipients for this letter, but it's likely that this letter was actually written to the Christians in several cities (including Ephesus) in a wider region of western Asia Minor (modern-day Turkey). Paul's letters were customarily copied and circulated among the cities throughout the regions where they were sent.

It's interesting to note that at the end of Paul's letter to the Colossians (which he wrote from prison at about the same time he wrote Ephesians), he writes:

> And when this letter has been read among you, have it also read in the church of the Laodiceans; and see that you also read the letter from Laodicea (Colossians 4:16).

The city of Laodicea was not far from Ephesus, and the letter Paul mentions, the letter to the Laodiceans, is unknown to us today. It's intriguing to speculate that the letter we call Ephesians might in fact be the letter to the Laodiceans that Paul mentions in Colossians. In all probability, Ephesians was originally read in all the churches in western Asia Minor, including Ephesus and Laodicea, and this may account for the seemingly lost letter to the Laodiceans.

The fact that we do not know for certain to whom Ephesians was originally written does not take away from the message or the majesty of this book. It is clearly written by Paul under the inspiration of the Holy Spirit, and it sets forth some of Paul's most essential teaching on the nature of the church, the body of Christ.

The apostle Paul wrote this letter while he was imprisoned in Rome, probably around AD 62. Paul wrote the letters of Colossians and Philemon from prison at about the same time as this letter. He states the theme of the letter at the outset:

> Blessed be the God and Father of our Lord Jesus Christ, who has blessed us in Christ with every spiritual blessing in the heavenly places (1:3).

The theme is that God has blessed us with every spiritual blessing in the heavenly places, according to the riches of his grace. We should be careful to understand this phrase "the heavenly places," because it appears several times in Ephesians. The term *heavenly* does not refer specifically to heaven, our eternal destiny with Jesus. Later in Ephesians, Paul writes:

> For we do not wrestle against flesh and blood, but against the rulers, against the authorities, against the cosmic powers over this present darkness, against the spiritual forces of evil *in the heavenly places* (6:12).

Obviously, the place we know as heaven will not be the home of "the spiritual forces of evil." When Paul speaks of "the heavenly places" in Ephesians, he is talking about a spiritual realm. He is distinguishing between things that are earthly and things that belong to a spiritual reality—a reality that is invisible to us now, but very real. Our riches in Christ come from that invisible reality, and our spiritual struggle against Satan also involves the forces of that invisible reality—yet both the blessings and the struggle are very real to us here and now, in our earthly reality.

The term "heavenly places," referring to the realm of our Lord's power and glory as well as the spiritual realm of Satan's power, is also found in Ephesians 2:6 and 3:10. It would be a misconception to think of the heavenly realm as out there in the cosmos or on some distant planet. The "heavenly places" are right here on earth, and they affect events and human lives here on earth—yet the "heavenly places" are beyond the reach of our senses, and we cannot see them.

But the "rulers and authorities" of the heavenly places can see us! Paul tells us that one of the reasons for the existence of the church—for believers like you and me—is so that the "rulers and authorities" of that invisible realm can see God's wisdom manifested in our lives. Paul writes:

> To me, though I am the very least of all the saints, this grace was given, to preach to the Gentiles the unsearchable riches of Christ, and to bring to light for everyone what is the plan of the mystery hidden for ages in God who created all things, so that through the church the manifold wisdom of God might now be made known to the rulers and authorities in the heavenly places (3:8-10).

This passage suggests that God has a secret plan, a hidden mystery—and he is unfolding that plan through ordinary believers, you and me, and making the mystery of his hidden wisdom known to "the rulers and authorities in the heavenly places." We don't understand that secret plan, but isn't it exciting to know that God is using us as instruments of that plan? Isn't it amazing to think that God is using us to reveal his hidden wisdom to the angels in the invisible realm?

Our "heavenly banker"

I once heard a story from the Great Depression that illustrates a key principle in Ephesians. During the financial panic of the Depression, there was such a run on financial institutions that banks simply did not have the cash on hand to cover all their customers' deposits. As a result, many banks imposed a rule that depositors could withdraw only 10 percent of their savings.

One man, however, was a good friend of the bank manager. The manager allowed this man to come in after regular banking hours and withdraw all his savings. Because the man had a special relationship with the banker, he got all his money out. Many other depositors were not so fortunate.

You and I are like that one depositor. In the book of Ephesians, we learn that we have a special relationship with our heavenly Banker. God, our Father, invites us into the heavenly treasure house to collect all the blessings that are ours in Christ.

Look closely at the letter to the Ephesians and you'll see that the theme of God's riches comes up again and again:

- In 1:7, Paul writes of the riches of God's grace.
- In 3:8, he writes of the unsearchable riches of Christ.
- In 3:16, he writes of the riches of God's glory.
- The word *riches* is repeated five times throughout Ephesians.
- The word *grace* is repeated twelve times.
- The word *glory* is repeated six times.
- The word *fullness* is repeated four times.
- The words *in Christ* are repeated thirteen times.

Again and again throughout this brief yet profound letter, Paul, inspired by the Holy Spirit of God, shows us how the death and resurrection of Jesus Christ has opened wide the limitless treasure house of God. Through Christ, we have been granted access to the riches, the grace, the glory, and the fullness of God.

The story is told of Wilson Mizner, a struggling writer of the early twentieth century, who married a fabulously wealthy woman, Myra Yerkes. Much of her wealth was invested in a vast art collection. Soon after their wedding, Mizner was disappointed to learn that his new wife had put him on a strict allowance. To raise some cash, Mizner took down a painting from the wall of his wife's mansion and sold it. The painting was a version of *The Last Supper of Christ*. When his wife discovered the empty frame, she demanded to know what he had done with the masterpiece. "Some masterpiece!" Mizner replied. "I only got fifty dollars a plate!"

Because of the Lord's masterpiece of grace—not only his last supper, but his death and his resurrection—God welcomes us into his vast treasure house to share his limitless riches. In Ephesians, Paul reveals to us:

- the fullness of our inheritance in Christ
- the infinite power that is ours in Christ
- the inexhaustible grace that we have in Christ
- the glorious position that is ours in Christ

So turn the page and join me as we explore the riches of God's treasure house.

1

The Riches of God's Treasure House

Ephesians 1:3-14

If you were on a raft, adrift in the ocean, the cruelest irony of your predicament is that you could die of thirst while surrounded by an endless supply of water. If you drank the ocean water, you would actually become dehydrated.

Normally, there is a 0.9 percent salt concentration in your bloodstream. Ocean water, by contrast, contains about 3.5 percent dissolved salts. If you drink seawater, your body will react by pulling water out of your cells to flush the salt from your system, and that causes you to become dehydrated. Extreme dehydration damages organs, especially the brain, and quickly leads to death.

Our culture is like an ocean of salt water. We human beings are thirsty for purpose, meaning, self-acceptance, and a sense of belonging. We are surrounded by books, magazines, and TV shows with so-called experts promising us the answers we seek—but they are moral, spiritual, and cultural salt water. The more we drink from these experts, the thirstier we become. The very act of lapping up the values and answers of our culture leaves us even more thirsty and dissatisfied than before.

In John 7:38, Jesus tells us, "Whoever believes in me, as the Scripture has said, 'Out of his heart will flow rivers of living water.'" Rivers of refreshing water will spring up and flow from the lives of all those who truly place their trust in Jesus. If you thirst for purpose, meaning, self-acceptance, and belonging—*it's yours*. It's freely available to you. Drink to your soul's content! Unlike the salt water of this dying culture, the fresh, clear water of God's love and forgiveness always satisfies.

Paul, in the opening lines of Ephesians, describes to us the rich and satisfying blessings that are instantly ours the moment we place our trust in Jesus:

> Blessed be the God and Father of our Lord Jesus Christ, who has blessed us in Christ with every spiritual blessing in the heavenly places, even as he chose us in him before the foundation of the world, that we should be holy and blameless before him. In love he predestined us for adoption as sons through Jesus Christ, according to the purpose of his will, to the praise of his glorious grace, with which he has blessed us in the Beloved. In him we have redemption through his blood, the forgiveness of our trespasses, according to the riches of his grace, which he lavished upon us, in all wisdom and insight making known to us the mystery of his will, according to his purpose, which he set forth in Christ as a plan for the fullness of time, to unite all things in him, things in heaven and things on earth (1:3-10).

When we come to Christ, we instantly receive all of these spiritual blessings. We don't receive *some* of them or *part* of them or a *promise* that we will receive them in the future. We don't receive them conditionally or in stages or if we qualify. We immediately and fully have "every spiritual blessing in the heavenly places." We stand holy and blameless before God the Father. We are his adopted children. We instantly have redemption through the Lord's blood, and we are fully forgiven for our sins.

Why do we possess all of these blessings? Because of "the riches of his grace," which he has showered on us for no other reason than his extravagant love for us. The Creator of heaven and earth chose us, predestined us, and redeemed us. As we walk with him, he walks with us, comforting and blessing us, delivering and sustaining us.

In Ephesians 1, Paul invites us into the very throne room of God as he shows us the blessings God has stored up for us in his treasure house—blessings we already fully possess if we belong to Jesus Christ. If you are a Christian living in spiritual poverty right now, it's because you don't realize what is already yours in Christ. You have never discovered the contents of the heavenly treasure house.

That is Paul's reason for writing the letter to the Ephesians, and that is my reason for writing this book on Ephesians—to enable you to discover the spiritual blessings that are available to you right here, right now. Once you have seen the contents of God's treasure house, once you truly understand the blessings that are yours right now, your life will never be the same.

His adopted children

In our society, we sometimes hear people say, "He's just the *adopted* son of that couple. He's not their *real* child." In other words, people mistakenly put too much emphasis on biology and not enough on love. They dismiss the adopted child as a second-class child, whose status is somehow not as valid as that of the biological child. That is faulty and wrong thinking, and it's extremely hurtful to adoptive children. Ask any adoptive parent and he or she will tell you that adopted children are no less loved than biological children.

I know a man who is a father to nineteen children. "Fourteen of my children are adopted," he says, "but I forget which ones." And that's how God loves you and me. He has an only begotten Son, Jesus—and he has many, many adopted children. As Paul writes:

> even as he chose us in him before the foundation of the world, that we should be holy and blameless before him. In love he predestined us for adoption as sons through Jesus Christ, according to the purpose of his will, to the praise of his glorious grace, with which he has blessed us in the Beloved (1:4-6).

Adoption is a beautiful picture of God's sovereign grace. The child did not choose the parents. The parents chose the child. That's how God has placed us into a relationship with himself. We did not choose him. He chose us.

An adoptive parent can give a child love, a nurturing home, and treatment that is fully equal to that given the biological children. An adoptive parent can even endow an adopted child with an inheritance. But when God adopts us, he gives us something no earthly adoptive parent can give a child: He gives us his very nature.

When God adopted us in Christ, he didn't merely bless us with love and care, forgiveness and grace, eternal life and an eternal inheritance. He imparted his very nature to us. When God adopts us, his act of adoption is a supernatural act. We take on the nature of Jesus. We become like him. We become what he is.

No, we do not instantly attain Christlike moral and spiritual perfection. But at the moment we place our trust in Christ, we become new creations. As Paul writes, "Therefore, if anyone is in Christ, he is a new creation. The old has passed away; behold, the new has come" (2 Corinthians 5:17). What is this new nature God gave us at the moment of our conversion? Paul writes: "For those whom he foreknew he also predestined to be conformed to the image of his

Son, in order that he might be the firstborn among many brothers" (Romans 8:29).

Jesus is God's firstborn—and you and I are the Lord's brothers and sisters, the adopted children of God the Father.

According to his riches

Before our heavenly Father adopted us, he paid the ultimate price. He bought us with the precious blood of his only Son, Jesus Christ:

> In him we have redemption through his blood, the forgiveness of our trespasses, according to the riches of his grace (1:7).

We were like slaves, owned and oppressed by a wicked slave-master called sin. Jesus paid the price in full for our deliverance from sin. And he paid that price in accordance with his riches.

If I ask a millionaire for a donation to support the work of a Christian ministry, and the millionaire writes a check for a hundred dollars, he has given a donation out of his riches—*but he has not given according to his riches*. He gave me an amount that is so small, compared with his wealth, that he will never miss it. But if that same millionaire would respond by writing a check for a *million* dollars, he would be giving according to his riches.

How rich is God? Look again at verse 3: "Blessed be the God and Father of our Lord Jesus Christ, who has blessed us in Christ with every spiritual blessing in the heavenly places." He possesses all conceivable blessings in the vast, limitless heavenly realms. Everything that exists belongs to him. And when he gave the infinitely precious blood of Jesus to redeem us from death, he truly gave according to his infinite riches. He held nothing back. The death of Christ was not a donation. It was the ultimate sacrifice. Paul goes on to write of God's grace:

> which he lavished upon us, in all wisdom and insight making known to us the mystery of his will, according to his purpose, which he set forth in Christ as a plan for the fullness of time, to unite all things in him, things in heaven and things on earth (1:8-10).

What does Paul mean when he says that God "lavished" his grace upon us? This word *lavished* is a powerful, intense word. It means that God poured all of his grace out upon us, freely and extravagantly. His grace is as endless as the ocean, as vast as the universe. His grace is inexhaustible. We can never outstrip God of his grace. It knows no end, no limit, no boundary.

What is the difference between a habitually sinning believer and a habitually sanctified believer who is becoming more like Christ every day? The difference is essentially this: The sinning believer does not understand the lavishness of God's grace and simply wants to take advantage of it, trampling God's love underfoot. The sanctified believer understands the lavish grace of God and is so filled with wonder and gratitude that the very idea of sinning against God's grace horrifies him and deters him from sinning. Let us not lose sight of the lavish grace of God!

Paul goes on to tell us about "the mystery of [God's] will, according to his purpose, which he set forth in Christ as a plan for the fullness of time" (1:9-10). God has a plan for the universe that is a mystery beyond our understanding—and his eternal plan includes a plan for your life and mine. He has given us key roles in furthering his eternal plan for heaven and earth, yet that plan is beyond our limited comprehension.

We are like an Allied soldier landing on the beach at Normandy on D-Day in June 1944. The soldier doesn't know all of the details of General Eisenhower's master plan for the invasion and liberation of Europe—the grand scheme of the invasion is a mystery to him. But that soldier has his orders, and he knows what he has to do in order to take the beach. By carrying out his individual role, he helps to fulfill the master plan.

God has a master plan for all of history that is beyond our comprehension. Paul calls God's incomprehensible plan "the mystery of his will, according to his purpose, which he set forth in Christ as a plan for the fullness of time, to unite all things in him, things in heaven and things on earth."

You and I have our jobs to do, our roles to fulfill, and as we do God's will for our lives, we play our part in carrying out the mystery of God's will, his plan for the fullness of time. Most amazing of all, God is "making known to us" this incomprehensible "mystery of his will." He reveals to us the part we play in his master plan, and that is what gives our lives meaning.

So if you are thirsty for purpose, meaning, self-acceptance, and a sense of belonging in life, here is the truth that satisfies. The moment you place your trust in Christ, you receive the spiritual blessing not only of redemption and forgiveness, not only adoption as a child of God, but a meaningful and significant part to play in God's eternal plan for the universe.

The guarantee of our inheritance

The story is told of a man named Jack Wurm who walked along a beach near San Francisco in 1949. He had lost his job as a restaurant worker and was completely out of money. Looking along the beach, he saw the waves wash a bottle onto the shore. Looking closer, he found that the tightly corked bottle had a message inside.

Upon opening the bottle, Wurm read: "To avoid any confusion, I leave my entire estate to the lucky person who finds this bottle, and to my attorney, Barry Cohen, share and share alike.—Daisy Alexander, June 20, 1937."

Jack Wurm investigated and found that the note had in fact been written by Daisy Singer Alexander, an heiress to the Singer sewing machine fortune. She had tossed the bottle off a bridge into the River Thames in England, and it had floated out to sea and bobbed along on the currents for some twelve years, drifting halfway around the world. By picking up that bottle, Jack Wurm received half of a $12 million estate.

To be sure, our inheritance was not by happenstance, but the point is well taken. In Ephesians 1, Paul writes:

> In him we have obtained an inheritance, having been predestined according to the purpose of him who works all things according to the counsel of his will, so that we who were the first to hope in Christ might be to the praise of his glory. In him you also, when you heard the word of truth, the gospel of your salvation, and believed in him, were sealed with the promised Holy Spirit, who is the guarantee of our inheritance until we acquire possession of it, to the praise of his glory (1:11-14).

When we come to Christ, we receive an inheritance far greater than what was left through a message in a bottle. And we don't just receive half an inheritance. We receive all of it, all at once.

Why has God given us this inheritance? Because we have been "predestined according to the purpose of him who works all things according to the counsel of his will." Before the earth was even formed, God looked along the corridor of time and said, "You are the object of my love. You are the object of my grace. You are the object of my mercy. You are the object of my redemption. You are the object of my blessing. You are my choice."

He made this decision about you sovereignly, but not arbitrarily. The sovereign predestination of the believer is another one of God's deep mysteries, which is revealed to us not only in New Testament passages such as Ephesians 1:11, but also in the Old Testament, as in the words of the psalmist:

For you formed my inward parts;
you knitted me together in my mother's womb...
Your eyes saw my unformed substance;
in your book were written, every one of them,
the days that were formed for me,
when as yet there was none of them.
(Psalm 139:13,16)

God formed us in our mothers' wombs. He willed it that we would be his children, adopted by grace through the sacrifice of his Son. He willed all the events of our lives so that we might come to him and believe in him. God's love for us is so unbelievable that he had to give us a supernatural gift of faith, sealed by the Holy Spirit, so that we could believe it. As Paul put it, "when you heard the word of truth, the gospel of your salvation, and believed in him, [you] were sealed with the promised Holy Spirit."

God gave us grace so that we wouldn't resist his overtures toward us. He opened our spiritual eyes so that we would recognize our desperate need for him. When we came to him, he assured us in his Word that it was not by accident that we belong to him—he chose us and adopted us. And that's not all.

God "has blessed us in Christ with every spiritual blessing in the heavenly places." What are some of these blessings he has given us?

He anticipated that we would need his peace. He does not make us grovel and beg for peace. He has already given us his peace through his Son, Jesus. As Jesus himself said in John 14:27, "Peace I leave with you; my peace I give to you. Not as the world gives do I give to you. Let not your hearts be troubled, neither let them be afraid."

God also knew that we would need joy in our lives. He knew that when we face trials in life, when the walls of opposition are closing in on us, when we go through times of confusion and doubt, we need his joy. We don't have to beg him for that joy. We need only accept the joy he freely gives us. As Jesus said in John 15:11, "These things I have spoken to you, that my joy may be in you, and that your joy may be full."

He knew we would need strength in our lives—strength for our times of loneliness, failure, defeat, exhaustion, and desperation. He didn't want us to have to beg for his strength. We are his children, and he loves us with an everlasting love. So, as Paul reminds us in Philippians 4:13, God has given us all the strength we need through his Son, Jesus: "I can do all things through him who strengthens me."

Sometimes we beg God for the blessings he has already given us. We fail to claim what is already ours through Christ. We fail to appreciate and appropriate his blessings to us. We forget to delight in his promises. But that doesn't mean God has not given us these blessings. It means we need to enter his treasure house and remind ourselves of all that is ours through Jesus Christ. We need to spend more time in Ephesians.

When we are tempted to forget God's blessings to us, we need to return to Ephesians 1:3 and hear again what Paul is saying to us: "Blessed be the God and Father of our Lord Jesus Christ, who has blessed us in Christ with every spiritual blessing in the heavenly places." Paul does not tell us that God *may* bless us, or he *can* bless us if we pray hard enough, or he *will* bless us sometime in the distant future. Paul says that God *has blessed us in Christ*—and not with a few dribs and drabs of blessing, but *with every spiritual blessing*.

In times of trouble, we simply need to praise God for every spiritual blessing because those blessings are already ours. But is that how we pray? When trouble comes, our prayers sound more like this: "Get me out of this trouble, God! Please, God! Please, please, please! I'll be good. I'll do favors for you. I'll stop swearing, and I'll stop fudging on my taxes, and I'll even put more money in the offering plate, God—if you'll just get me out of this trouble!" We think we can bargain with God or appease God and coax him into serving our needs.

But Paul describes a far different attitude that we should have when we face times of trial and trouble. Our prayer should sound more like this: "Lord, you know the trouble I'm facing. But Lord, you promised in your Word, 'Let not your hearts be troubled. Believe in God; believe also in me.' Lord, I have complete confidence that you have already blessed me in Christ with every spiritual blessing in the heavenly places. You have already given me the strength and the power to deal with any trial I may face. Lord, I know that you are walking with me, and I look forward to seeing how you are going to meet my needs through this situation. Lord, in you I have everything I need. In the powerful name of Jesus, amen."

The difference between these two prayers is the assurance we find in Ephesians 1—the assurance that God "has blessed us in Christ with every spiritual blessing in the heavenly places."

To the praise of his glory

Why has he blessed us with every spiritual blessing? Why has he chosen us before the foundation of the world? Why has he adopted us as his children? Why has he redeemed us and paid a hefty price of his own blood for us? Why has he lavished his forgiveness on us? Why does he continuously pour his grace upon us? Why does he give us wisdom and insight according to his infinite riches? Verses 12 through 14 give us the answer.

> so that we who were the first to hope in Christ might be to the praise of his glory. In him you also, when you heard the word of truth, the gospel of your salvation, and believed in him, were sealed with the promised Holy Spirit, who is the guarantee of our inheritance until we acquire possession of it, to the praise of his glory (1:12-14).

Twice in these verses Paul uses the expression "to the praise of his glory." What does this mean? It means that God has blessed us, saved us, adopted us, redeemed us, lavished grace on us, and made known to us the mystery of his will so that we would live in a state of worship and praise at all times, in every aspect of our lives. Regardless of the difficulties we may face, our homes should be sanctuaries of praise to God. Regardless of problem situations and problem people, our workplaces ought to be sanctuaries of continual praise to God. Everywhere we go, we should bless others with praise to the One who has blessed us with every spiritual blessing.

We will continue to praise God throughout eternity. As Paul writes in Romans 8:17, as God's children we are "heirs of God and fellow heirs with Christ." What's more, we will become Christ's inheritance so that we may worship and praise him at all times. The praise of his glory goes on and on—both here and in heaven.

During World War II, the government issued war bonds to fund the war effort. Millions of people bought war bonds to support their country, and the government promised to repay that investment with interest. But years later, when those bonds reached maturity, half a billion dollars' worth of war bonds were not redeemed and all of that money went unclaimed. This is the equivalent of more than $13 billion today.

Were the unredeemed bonds lost? Were they destroyed? Did people simply put the bonds away and forget them? Were they inherited and were the heirs ignorant of their worth? We can only guess.

God's treasure house is filled with blessing, strength, and power for our lives. Let's be aware of these riches and claim them every day. What a waste it would be to go a single day without claiming the rich reward of God's treasure house. Don't claim one, don't claim some—claim *every spiritual blessing* in the heavenly places.

2

You Have All You Need

Ephesians 1:15-23

For most of my life, I enjoyed twenty-twenty vision in both eyes. I would sometimes brag about my eyesight, especially when people younger than me began wearing pharmacy reading glasses. I confidently said, "I'll never need those. I have twenty-twenty vision."

One day when I was forty-seven, I was having my daily devotional time, and I noticed something was wrong with my reading lamp. It was hard to read the print in my Bible. Just the day before, I had read from the same Bible without any trouble at all. The change was so sudden, I knew it had to be a problem with the reading lamp.

It was a three-way lamp, so I tried all three settings—yet I still found it difficult to make out the print on the page. Perhaps the bulb was growing dim. I tried changing the lightbulb, but the new bulb was just as defective as the old one. I tried turning on all of the lights in the room. It was as bright as the noonday sun in that room, and I still struggled to read the print in my Bible.

A week later, I talked to an eye doctor friend and said, "There's something wrong with my eyes. I need to make an appointment and have you do a complete check of my eyes. I think I'm developing glaucoma or some other serious eye disease."

"You don't need to make an appointment," he said. "That would be a waste of time. Just go to the pharmacy and buy some reading glasses—get the lowest power of magnification. I think you'll find that's all you need."

"Oh, I don't need reading glasses," I said. "I have twenty-twenty vision. This has to be something serious."

"Well, just try the pharmacy glasses and see what happens. If they don't solve your problem, you can come to the office and I'll check your eyes."

So I went to the local store and bought some reading glasses—and what a difference those glasses made!

The problem was not in the lightbulb or the reading lamp. There was nothing wrong with the way the Bible was printed. The problem was in my eyes all along. The muscles in my eyes had weakened due to age, and the change came so suddenly that I was quick to blame everything but my own eyes.

One of the key themes of Paul in Ephesians is: Don't go looking to outside sources for more power and more resources. If you think you lack God's power, if you think you lack God's resources, it's because you fail to see clearly what is already yours. You don't need more power, more strength, more faith, more joy, more anything. You have already been blessed with every spiritual blessing. You just need to have these blessings brought into focus so you can see more clearly what you already have.

Paul's prayer for the Ephesians

Paul offers a prayer of thanks for the believers who demonstrated great faith in the Lord and great love toward one another:

> For this reason, because I have heard of your faith in the Lord Jesus and your love toward all the saints, I do not cease to give thanks for you, remembering you in my prayers, that the God of our Lord Jesus Christ, the Father of glory, may give you the Spirit of wisdom and of revelation in the knowledge of him (1:15-17).

Not only does Paul give thanks for these believers, but he prays on their behalf—"remembering you in my prayers." Paul did not say, "I've asked God to give you more strength and power." And he did not say, "I've asked God to shower you with more blessings." And he did not say, "I prayed that God would continue doling out your inheritance to you, a little at a time in weekly installments. Every Sunday when you go to church, you'll get a little more of your inheritance in Christ."

No, Paul prayed that these believers would *know what they already have*. He prayed that God "may give you a spirit of wisdom and of revelation in the knowledge of him."

Many years ago, I talked to a friend in Texas, an entrepreneur who was involved in many different businesses. He told me, "I have so many companies and holdings that I don't know them all. One day I'm going to sit down with my advisors and have them help me put my arms around everything I own."

In a spiritual sense, that is Paul's prayer for these believers. He prays that we would have the wisdom and comprehension to know what we already possess in Christ so that we can put our arms around everything we own. We have been blessed with every spiritual blessing in the heavenly realms. That's why it takes divine wisdom and divine intervention for us to comprehend all we have in Christ Jesus.

Many people mistakenly believe that the words "Know thyself" come from the Bible. Those words are not found anywhere in the Bible. They come from ancient Greek philosophy, and have been attributed to Heraclitus, Pythagoras, Socrates, and others. History records that "Know thyself" was inscribed in stone in the forecourt of the Temple of Apollo at Delphi. Our culture today remains obsessed with the imperative to "Know thyself." One of the most popular magazines in America is *Self*, which informs readers of all the latest ways to beautify, nourish, exercise, glorify, trim, tone, and gratify the self.

I have learned that I don't need to spend any time or money getting to know myself. I already know myself. I can tell you everything anyone needs to know about myself in three sentences:

- I was lost and now I'm found.
- I was blind, but now I see.
- I was a nobody, but now I am a child of the King.

That is all I need to know about myself. And once I know all I need to know about myself, I simply have to live in accord with what I know. I committed my life to Jesus Christ back in the mid-sixties. In all the years since then, I have been learning about every blessing that is mine in Christ—and I keep discovering new blessings I didn't know I had! With every new blessing I discover, I realize I haven't even scratched the surface of all the blessings I possess in Christ.

Many Christians today chase after every new idea that emerges on the evangelical landscape, hoping to find the secret to the deeper life, the higher life, or the happy life. One recent movement in the church has hundreds of thousands of people following it and millions of dollars spent on it—and it is a heresy. This movement teaches that God takes risks and you should too. Think for a moment how absurd this idea is. The omniscient God, the all-powerful God, the omnipresent God, the God who knew the future of the universe before time began—this God took risks?

Our God is not a cosmic gambler, but the Lord of time and space. Almighty sovereign Jehovah does not toss the dice. He speaks, and every subatomic particle in the universe obeys.

Paul wants us to know that we do not need to chase after the latest spiritual fads and fashions. We simply need the wisdom to recognize the blessings we already have and the obedience to put them to good use.

I've often heard Christians lament, "If only the Lord would bless me. Why does he withhold his blessing from me?" Yet the people who say that have *already* been blessed with every spiritual blessing in the heavenly places. We do not lack blessings as followers of Christ. Our real problem is that our blessings are so vast that we cannot get our arms around them. Only the Holy Spirit himself can enable us to understand the vastness of our blessings in Christ. As Paul writes in another letter:

> But, as it is written,
> "What no eye has seen, nor ear heard,
> nor the heart of man imagined,
> what God has prepared for those who love him."
> (1 Corinthians 2:9)

Most Christians, reading those words, think that Paul is talking about heaven. And heaven is certainly *part* of what God has prepared for us who love him. But God has also prepared wonders and blessings for us to enjoy in the here and now.

Why is it important that we grasp the incredible blessings God has given us? It's important because it's impossible to live a life of obedience until we truly comprehend who we are in Christ. It's impossible to live a fulfilled, joyful, contented life until you begin to grasp what Paul is praying for.

When I was young and inclined to get into mischief, my parents told me, "Remember who you are, Michael. Remember your family's name and reputation. Remember, remember, remember." When I followed their advice, when I remembered my identity as a member of the Youssef family, I was less inclined to mischief. When I got into trouble, it was often because I had lost sight of my family identity.

In much the same way, Paul tells us in Ephesians, "It's easy to forget who you are and the blessings you already have, so I'm praying that God the Father of our Lord Jesus Christ may give you the Spirit of wisdom and of revelation in the knowledge of him." Only the Spirit can reveal these blessings, so Paul's prayer was of the utmost importance. It's a model prayer that you and I would do well to emulate for ourselves and others.

Our emotions—the eyes of our hearts

What prevents us from understanding how God has blessed us with every spiritual blessing? The greatest barrier is our feelings—what Paul refers to as "the eyes of your hearts." He writes:

> having the eyes of your hearts enlightened, that you may know what is the hope to which he has called you, what are the riches of his glorious inheritance in the saints (1:18).

There's nothing wrong with feelings and emotions. There's nothing inherently evil about the eyes of our hearts. God gave us our emotions for a reason. We experience fear as a warning against danger. We experience anger as a protective mechanism, so that we will take action and ward off threats. We experience love and affection as a way of forming human bonds. We experience joy so that we can revel in the blessings God gives to us.

But emotions are variable and unreliable. They go up and down. Our emotions have a strong effect on the way we perceive the world. That's why Paul calls our emotions the eyes of our hearts. If we are sad, gloomy, bitter, or depressed, we filter everything that happens to us, including our relationship with God, through those negative emotions. In a negative emotional state, it's hard for us to sense God's blessings, and we easily fall into the trap of believing that God has not blessed us at all.

That's why Paul writes that we must have the eyes of our hearts *enlightened*—that is, illuminated and filled with the light of God's truth—so that we may know the hope to which he has called us, the riches of his glorious inheritance in the saints. Our emotional life must be balanced by the light of God's truth. And that means we must not only feel, but we must think clearly and rationally, and we must meditate on the truth of God's Word.

Feelings are wonderful in their proper place, but when feelings replace thinking, when feelings replace the truth of God's revealed Word, we lose sight of our blessings in Christ, and we invite disaster. But when our lives are ruled by the truth of God's Word, we see life as it really is. Either our emotions will distort God's truth, or God's truth will rule over our emotions.

Our feelings are a powerful ally when they are enlightened by God's truth. When we comprehend the truth about God's election and predestination of the believer, about God's adoption and redemption of the believer, about our inheritance in Christ, we feel emotionally lifted and we feel a deep sense of gratitude to God. When we understand that God is the one who called us, loved us, wooed us, reached down to us, and lifted us out of our sins, that blessed assurance will carry us through all the times when our emotions are too high or too low, times when we don't feel very spiritual, and even times when we don't feel saved at all.

Never confuse feelings with reality. And the spiritual reality that Paul reveals to us in Ephesians 1 is that, whether our feelings are high or low, hot or cold, God has blessed us in Christ with every spiritual blessing in the heavenly places. That is the enduring and indisputable truth that enlightens the eyes of our hearts.

The dynamite of God

In the next two verses, Paul describes for us God's "incomparably great power for us who believe," a power I call "the dynamite of God." Paul writes:

> and what is the immeasurable greatness of his power toward us who believe, according to the working of his great might that he worked in Christ when he raised him from the dead and seated him at his right hand in the heavenly places (1:19-20).

The original Greek word for "power" in verse 19 is *dunamis*, from which we get the word *dynamite*. So I think dynamite is an excellent metaphor to describe the power God gives us. Paul doesn't say that this power is given to us in installments. All the power we need has already been given to us—*BOOM!* It's here. It's ours. It's dynamic. It's explosive. We can't get any more of God's power than we already have. We simply need to be aware of what he has already given us. We need to comprehend that power and claim it in order to put it to good use.

Jesus told the disciples in Acts 1:8, "But you will receive power when the Holy Spirit has come upon you." If you have committed your life to Jesus Christ, you have already received that power. You don't have to wait for it. You don't have to work for it. It's yours.

Paul goes on to tell us in verse 20 that this is the same power that God used at the resurrection, the power "he worked in Christ when he raised him from the dead and seated him at his right hand in the heavenly places." That same power is yours and mine. He is pouring that power through us to raise us from the death of sin and to place us in the heavenlies—not just after we die but right here, right now. You may be sitting on your couch or in your easy chair as you read these words, but Paul wants you to know that, if you are in Christ, you are also sitting in the heavenlies.

In 1 Corinthians 6:3, Paul tells us that we are going to judge the angels. If we are going to judge heavenly powers and authorities, we had better start living as if we belong to the Lord Jesus Christ, not to this world. We had better start recognizing and utilizing our God-given power *now*. We need to use God's power to energize our witness and our ministry to the least and the lost. We need to use the *dunamis* power of God to energize our influence for God throughout our society.

I've met many Christians who hesitate to share their faith because they don't understand the power they possess in Christ. They think they need to lead people to Christ in their own strength, their own wisdom—and they feel inadequate to the task. And they are! No one can lead anyone to Christ in their own strength. Let's stop trying to do God's job. Let's simply be obedient to do what God has called us to do, and then let God energize our witness with his Spirit, his power, his *dunamis*.

We can't convert anyone. Only God converts people. We need only to touch people where they are, to love them where they are, and as we obey him, he will reveal the power of Christ in us.

Christ over all

Paul goes on to tell us that God has placed Jesus:

> far above all rule and authority and power and dominion, and above every name that is named, not only in this age but also in the one to come. And he put all things under his feet and gave him as head over all things to the church, which is his body, the fullness of him who fills all in all (1:21-23).

God's power has placed Jesus above all rule and authority and power and dominion, and above every name that is named. God has placed his Son not merely a notch above all power and dominion, but *far* above those powers. One thousand years before Christ, the psalmist predicted that God would place all things under the feet of Jesus, making even his enemies his footstool (see Psalm 110:1).

This truth can be understood only through the enlightening power of the Holy Spirit. The natural mind can't comprehend it. To the world, Jesus was just a good man, a great moral teacher, a role model of love and self-sacrifice. But through the power of the Holy Spirit, you and I understand the great truth that Jesus sits on the rim of the universe with authority and power. He is far above every name that is named, not only in this age but also in the ages to come. He rules over powers, authorities, nations, dominions, kings, presidents, dictators, angels, devils, believers, and scoffers. He rules over his children and the church. He is over everything.

The world does not know it yet, but the Lord Jesus has already been crowned in heaven as the one true God. We can't see his glory with our physical eyes, even with twenty-twenty vision. But we can see with the enlightened eyes of the heart, as the Spirit gives us light. The head and ruler of the church is Jesus Christ—and not only that, but the head and ruler of this world and the entire universe is Jesus Christ.

Without Jesus, the church, the body of believers, would be a dead and lifeless institution, because Christ and Christ alone fills the church with power. This is why so many churches actually *do* appear dead and lifeless—Christ does not empower churches that do not preach the truth and do not worship him in truth. Some churches have thousands of members, but they have no life because they do not have the power of Christ.

The day is coming when every knee shall bow and every tongue confess that Jesus Christ is Lord, to the glory of God the Father (see Philippians 2:10-11). In that day, only the works we have done in the power of Jesus will stand. May the power of Christ explode from our lives. May the reality of Christ be revealed through your life and mine. May the power of Christ be manifested in our daily lives, in everything we do and say.

3

Your Heavenly Citizenship

Ephesians 2

In 1977 I came to the United States from Australia on a student visa so I could pursue my graduate studies here. Later, I obtained what was then called a "legal alien visa." Though I lived in America, I was a noncitizen, so I did not have the rights and benefits of citizenship. The government could take away my resident status at any time, and I could be deported. I could not vote or run for political office. I could not be protected by the U.S. government when I traveled abroad.

But in 1984, I became a citizen and was given all the rights and privileges the U.S. government offers its citizens, with one important exception—and I'm *not* referring to the "natural born citizen" clause in Article II of the Constitution, which bars me from running for president. I'll tell you what that privilege is at the end of the chapter.

The benefits of citizenship, which many Americans take for granted, are truly amazing. As a citizen, I can come into the U.S.

and go out of the U.S. as I please. I have U.S. embassy protection abroad. I can never be deported from the United States. I can run for any political office, except that of president of the United States. I can vote for the candidate of my choice. And the list goes on and on.

Citizenship makes a huge difference. All of these benefits are mine even if I travel overseas. The key to my rights as a citizen is not where I happen to be living, but what citizenship I hold.

The free gift of resurrection power

In a similar (yet far more significant) way, the apostle Paul says in Ephesians 2 that there were some who were near to Christ by virtue of the old covenant (he is speaking of the Jews, God's chosen people), and there were some who were far from Christ and who knew nothing about the Messiah (he is speaking of the Gentiles). But neither the Jews nor the Gentiles could hold heavenly citizenship apart from Jesus Christ.

The Jews were like the resident aliens. The Gentiles were like the aliens living overseas. Neither were citizens. Neither could enjoy the benefits of citizenship.

Being near to Christ as a Jew makes no difference. Being far from Christ as a Gentile makes no difference. Only one condition grants you all the benefits of citizenship in the Lord's kingdom: Jesus Christ must become your Savior and Lord. You must be a believer and follower of Christ in order to gain access to his amazing treasure house and receive the blessings and benefits of that treasure house.

Paul begins chapter 2 by reminding us of who and what we were before we received Christ as our Lord and Savior:

> And you were dead in the trespasses and sins in which you once walked, following the course of this world, following the prince of the power of the air, the spirit that is now at work in the sons of disobedience—among whom we all once lived in the passions of our flesh, carrying out

> the desires of the body and the mind, and were by nature children of wrath, like the rest of mankind (2:1-3).

There is a big lie that permeates all religions *except* Christianity. This lie says that if you are a good person, you will go to heaven. Genuine biblical Christianity does not teach this lie. The Bible tells us that when each one of us was born, our spirits were dead. We cared more about ourselves than God—or anybody else. If you are not alive in Christ, you are dead in sin.

We see this principle illustrated in the Lord's parable of the loving father and the prodigal son. When the son returned home in repentance, his father joyously announced, "For this my son was dead, and is alive again; he was lost, and is found" (Luke 15:24a).

The condition of every human being, apart from faith in Christ, is spiritual death. Everyone who lives without Christ suffers from spiritual death. Like a corpse, the person without Christ is blind to the Lord's glory, deaf to his voice, unfeeling toward his love, and unresponsive to his leading.

People don't like to think of themselves as dead and unresponsive. We all like to think that we pay our own way, we've earned what we have, we've worked hard for everything we have—even our salvation, our place in heaven. But we can't earn salvation. We can't work our way to heaven. We can receive salvation only as a free gift. God did it all.

Why can't we earn our own salvation? Because we are dead in our sins. A corpse can't work. A corpse can't pay. A corpse can do nothing. That's why salvation is a free gift from God. Nothing less than the gift of God's resurrection power can save us.

God's purpose for your life

If a drunk driver hits and kills a child, there is nothing he can do to make it up to the grieving parents. No matter how many times he says, "I'm sorry, I'm sorry," no matter how much money he offers, he cannot assuage their grief or his guilt. There is only one way that there can be a relationship between this offender and the grieving parents: The parents must freely offer him their forgiveness.

By our very nature and inclination, we have offended God. We cannot make it up to God. We can't do anything to expunge our guilt before him. The only way there can be a relationship between God and us is if God himself offers us his mercy and forgiveness. So Paul writes:

> But God, being rich in mercy, because of the great love with which he loved us… (2:4).

God, who was offended by our rejection of him and our defiance toward him, is so rich in mercy and love that he not only forgave us, but he sent his only Son, Jesus, to die for us. As a result, God moved us from death to life:

> even when we were dead in our trespasses, [God] made us alive together with Christ—by grace you have been saved— (2:5).

When you came to Jesus Christ, confessing and repenting and inviting him into your life, he performed spirit-to-spirit resuscitation on you. He breathed life into your dead spirit. At that point, for the first time in your life, you became alive and responsive to God. Paul tells us what happened as a result:

> and raised us up with him and seated us with him in the heavenly places in Christ Jesus, so that in the coming ages he might show the immeasurable riches of his grace in kindness toward us in Christ Jesus (2:6-7).

The life that God breathed into us has a purpose. Our purpose is to live this life with heaven in mind. We are to live as ambassadors of our heavenly home. Why? Because we are already seated in heaven, and we are representatives of our new citizenship in heaven.

C.S. Lewis got tired of hearing people say that Christians are so heavenly minded that they are of no earthly good. So in *Mere Christianity*, he wrote:

> If you read history you will find that the Christians who did most for the present world were just those who thought most of the next. The Apostles themselves, who set on foot the conversion of the Roman Empire, the great men who built up the Middle Ages, the English Evangelicals who abolished the Slave Trade, all left their mark on Earth, precisely because their minds were occupied with Heaven. It is since Christians have largely ceased to think of the other world that they have become so ineffective in this [world].[1]

Heavenly minded people accomplish great things for God here on earth. God has given us good works to do. If we are truly heavenly minded, we will obediently and joyfully fulfill that role and accomplish that work. As Paul writes:

> For by grace you have been saved through faith. And this is not your own doing; it is the gift of God, not a result of works, so that no one may boast. For we are his workmanship, created in Christ Jesus for good works, which God prepared beforehand, that we should walk in them (2:8-10).

Understand, we are not saved *by* our good works. Rather, we are created *for* good works. No good work, no matter how beneficial or sacrificial it may be, can earn us our salvation. But as people who have been saved by God's grace, we joyfully and gratefully carry out the good works God has given us. We obey him out of gratitude, not out of fear or a desire to earn our way to heaven.

Salvation is by grace through faith, not by works. Salvation is God's gift to us. If we could earn salvation, then God would owe it to us. But God doesn't owe us anything. He gives us everything as a free gift of his grace. Now *we owe him everything* because of our endless gratitude for his amazing gift. Out of the depths of our gratitude, we do good works—the works he created us to do.

God has a job for every one of his children. If you are not exercising the spiritual gifts God has given you, then you are not doing the good works you were created to do. Every human being on planet Earth was created by God, and those who are in Christ have been recreated and restored to life by God. He has remolded our spirits. He has refashioned our hearts. He has reshaped our minds.

God created us physically, and he re-created us spiritually so that we may accomplish his purpose for our lives. He calls each of his sons and daughters to know him—and to make him known.

A heavenly citizenship

We were all born into a state of complete separation from God. The Gentiles, of course, had a bigger separation from God than the Jews because the Jews, at least, were taught to anticipate the coming of the Messiah. Paul writes:

> Therefore remember that at one time you Gentiles in the flesh, called "the uncircumcision" by what is called the circumcision, which is made in the flesh by hands—remember that you were at that time separated from Christ, alienated from the commonwealth of Israel and strangers to the covenants of promise, having no hope and without God in the world. But now in Christ Jesus you who once were far off have been brought near by the blood of Christ (2:11-13).

The Old Testament is filled with promises and a sense of anticipation of the coming Messiah. The Jews were closer to God by virtue of the Abrahamic covenant, and the Gentiles were far away from God. In terms of our U.S. citizenship analogy, the Jews were like aliens who live in the United States, while the Gentiles were like the alien residents who reside outside the United States. Neither are citizens, though one group is nearer than the other.

The lower Mississippi River is more than a mile wide at many points. Could anyone jump across the Mississippi River? An Olympic long jumper might be able to jump twenty-five feet or more, but if he were to try to jump across the Mississippi, he would end up in the river, far short of the other bank. An average person might be able to jump five or even ten feet, but his jump would end in the river as well. Some people can jump farther than others, but no one can jump all the way across the Mississippi River.

If you want to cross the river, you've got to stop trying to jump it in your own strength. Only a boat or an airplane can take you all the way across the river.

And if you want to become a citizen of heaven, you've got to stop trying to get there in your own strength. Only Jesus can enable those who are near and those who are far to become citizens of heaven. Only he can give you heavenly citizenship. As Paul writes to the Gentile believers:

> For he himself is our peace, who has made us both one and has broken down in his flesh the dividing wall of hostility by abolishing the law of commandments expressed in ordinances, that he might create in himself one new man in place of the two, so making peace, and might reconcile us both to God in one body through the cross, thereby killing the hostility. And he came and preached peace to you who were far off and peace to those who were near (2:14-17).

Sin causes strife, hatred, bitterness, and conflict. The solution to the disharmony of sin is the peace that comes from the shed blood of Christ, which removes our sin.

Wherever there is strife between a husband and wife, between two brothers in Christ, between two sisters in Christ, between two family members or church members, it is because Jesus does not reign supreme in their relationship. Sin has taken the place of Christ.

Someone may say, "I am a Christian and my spouse is a Christian, but our home is a war zone." If that is the case, it's because you have allowed sin to control you. And when sin dominates, the Holy Spirit grieves over your home and your heart.

In the ancient temple of Jerusalem, the priests had posted signs in both Greek and Latin that read, "No Gentile may enter beyond the dividing wall into the court around the Holy Place. Whoever is caught will be to blame for his subsequent death."

Today, there are many homes, many hearts, and many lives with similar signs hanging on them. The signs are invisible, but the message is clear: "Do not enter. Leave me in my isolation. You and I are at war."

Jesus breaks down the barriers that separate us. He brings peace and reconciliation to our relationships. Even historic hostilities between Jews and Gentiles have been demolished in him. When Christ reigns supreme, all hatred, prejudice, and strife must cease, because he is our peace. When he comes in and reigns over our hearts and lives, there is peace and unity.

A new kind of family

When Jesus abolished hostility between us and his heavenly Father, he also abolished hostility between believers. The dividing wall of hostility and separation has fallen between Jew and Gentile, between white and black and brown, between old and young, between men and women, between rich and poor, between Democrat and Republican, between those who squeeze the middle of the toothpaste tube and those who squeeze the tube from the end. All of these barriers and hostilities are shattered by Christ.

Jesus has formed a whole new *kind* of family. It's a *heavenly* family with God as our Father and with our fellow believers as brothers and sisters who have heavenly blood flowing through their veins. Paul writes:

> For through him we both have access in one Spirit to the Father. So then you are no longer strangers and aliens, but you are fellow citizens with the saints and members of the household of God, built on the foundation of the apostles and prophets, Christ Jesus himself being the cornerstone, in whom the whole structure, being joined together, grows into a holy temple in the Lord. In him you also are being built together into a dwelling place for God by the Spirit (2:18-22).

Jesus tells us in Matthew 18:15 that if we have an offense against another believer, we must go to the offending brother or sister because we are a family. And if Jesus is presiding over his family, then peace must reign supreme. Your love in Christ must transcend your disagreements.

Because of Christ, we now have a home—a place of belonging—where Christ himself is the foundation. Without a foundation, a house will not stand for very long. With Jesus as the foundation and the cornerstone, the One who supports the entire structure, the house can never fall. The structure of the house—its walls and roof—are made up of God's Word as recorded by the Old Testament prophets and the New Testament apostles. This is the house where the truth of God's Word dwells and reigns supreme.

The Word of God reigns over our thoughts and over our emotions. It reigns over our relationships in our families—and in the family of faith, the church. It reigns over our lives.

At the beginning of this chapter, I talked about the benefits of U.S. citizenship. I said there is one place where U.S. citizenship cannot help the naturalized immigrant. If the naturalized immigrant goes back to the country of his birth, he is often viewed as a citizen of that country, not a citizen of the United States, and he is treated by that country as one who is subject to its laws, not the laws of the United States. The naturalized immigrant's country of birth frequently has no regard for his adopted U.S. citizenship.

And there is a spiritual analogy here: Whenever we deliberately go back to sin and rebellion, we remove ourselves from the protective covering of our heavenly citizenship. We are still citizens of heaven. We are still members of our adopted heavenly country. We are still saved eternally. Our names are permanently written in the Book of Life—and it is written with the indelible blood of Christ. We are still justified before God.

But we bring pain on ourselves when we deliberately wander away from all the benefits of the treasure house. Friend in Christ, do not surrender the blessings and benefits of your heavenly citizenship. If you have wandered in a spiritual wilderness, it's time for you to turn and repent. Leave that wilderness. Return to the place of your true citizenship.

Come home.

4

God's Perspective on Life

Ephesians 3

In Florence, Italy, in the 1400s, painters made a discovery that revolutionized the art world. The discovery was called *perspective*. Before this discovery, all paintings depicted flat, two-dimensional people against a flat, two-dimensional background. But with the discovery of perspective, paintings began to develop depth and realism. Objects in paintings could be seen to recede into the distance.

One of the leading painters of this period was Paolo Uccello. He became so fascinated with perspective that he would stay up all night working on drawings and paintings that used this new artistic concept. When Uccello's wife begged him to come to bed, he refused and responded, "What a delightful thing this perspective is!"

Not only do we need *visual* perspective but we also need *spiritual* perspective. We need to have God's view of life. In order to understand life and eternity, we need to see life from God's perspective, and we need to perceive God as he truly is.

If we perceive God as generous, merciful, and abounding in love, we will trust in his goodness and we will want to live in obedience to him. We'll want to please him because of our deep sense of gratitude and thanksgiving. We'll have a confidence and optimism about life because we will trust God to be in control of our circumstances.

But if we perceive God to be vengeful, unpredictable, unforgiving, and angry, we will resent him and fear him. If we obey him at all, it will be an obedience that comes from terror of punishment. We may outwardly obey, but we will inwardly rebel. We will go through our lives living in fear and pessimism, always expecting the worst from God and from our circumstances.

So much of how we live our lives depends on our perspective. The better we are able to see life from God's perspective, the more joyful and effective our lives will be. When we have God's perspective on life and its trials, we can trust God's purpose for our lives even when life isn't going well. We will start each day with a sense of anticipation of what God has planned for us. We won't allow fear to control us. We won't allow criticism to erode our confidence.

Looking at life from God's perspective, we know he loves us and is working all things together for his good purpose. That's why it's important that every Christian understands that he or she has a significant role in God's plan for history. The moment we say, "I don't matter to God," we not only make God out to be a liar, but we invite defeat and disaster into our own lives.

Show me a joyful, contented Christian, and I will show you a Christian who is obedient to the will of God. Show me a Christian who is not defeated by circumstances, and I will show you a Christian who understands his or her riches in Christ Jesus. That is a Christian who has God's perspective on life.

The mystery of Christ

Ephesians 1:3 is the foundational verse for the entire letter: "Blessed be the God and Father of our Lord Jesus Christ, who has blessed us in Christ with every spiritual blessing in the heavenly places." With that verse in mind, we come to Ephesians 3, where Paul tells us that we are not only to know that we possess every blessing in the heavenly places, but we are to put those blessings to good use. He shows us the conditions or qualifications for taking hold of and utilizing the blessings and benefits of God's treasure house. He begins:

> For this reason I, Paul, a prisoner for Christ Jesus on behalf of you Gentiles—assuming that you have heard of the stewardship of God's grace that was given to me for you, how the mystery was made known to me by revelation, as I have written briefly. When you read this, you can perceive my insight into the mystery of Christ, which was not made known to the sons of men in other generations as it has now been revealed to his holy apostles and prophets by the Spirit. This mystery is that the Gentiles are fellow heirs, members of the same body, and partakers of the promise in Christ Jesus through the gospel.
>
> Of this gospel I was made a minister according to the gift of God's grace, which was given me by the working of his power. To me, though I am the very least of all the saints, this grace was given, to preach to the Gentiles the unsearchable riches of Christ, and to bring to light for everyone what is the plan of the mystery hidden for ages in God who created all things, so that through the church the manifold wisdom of God might now be made known to the rulers and authorities in the heavenly places. This was according to the eternal purpose that he has realized in Christ Jesus our Lord, in whom we have boldness and access with confidence through our faith in him. So I ask you not to lose heart over what I am suffering for you, which is your glory (3:1-13).

Paul starts by saying, "For this reason I, Paul, a prisoner for Christ Jesus on behalf of you Gentiles—" And then he interrupts himself.

He is about to offer the prayer that begins at verse 14, but first he interrupts his introductory remarks and says, in effect, "Oh, before I get to the reason I kneel before the Father, I need to establish my credentials. I'm the one who was commissioned by Jesus to make the mystery of Christ known."

What is "the mystery of Christ"? It is the fact that in Christ, and Christ alone, Gentiles and Jews have equal standing with God. In Christ alone those who are far (the Gentiles) and those who are near (the Jews) can become citizens of heaven. Only in Christ can the hostility between human and God, and between different human individuals and groups, be abolished. Paul is explaining his mission, his calling, which is to reveal the mystery of Christ.

Why is that a mystery? The reconciliation of Jews and Gentiles was prophesied in the Old Testament, especially by the prophets Isaiah, Jeremiah, and Ezekiel. But God's chosen people did not understand these prophecies until Christ came. One of these prophecies was Isaiah 49:6, in which God says to the coming Messiah (who is Jesus):

> "I will make you as a light for the nations,
> that my salvation may reach to the end of the earth."

If you read this passage in its context, you see clearly that God states that he is sending the Messiah, Jesus, not only to the tribes of Israel, but to all the nations of the world. So Paul, in Ephesians 3:2-13, establishes his credentials as God's messenger to preach the good news to the Gentiles, who are "fellow heirs, members of the same body" along with the Jewish believers.

Paul's second prayer

In Ephesians 1:15-23, the apostle Paul offers a first prayer. He prays for the Ephesians that they may know the limitless resources they possess in Christ Jesus. Now, in Ephesians 3:14-21, Paul prays a second prayer. This second prayer is closely connected to the first.

In the first prayer, Paul prayed for the believers to know every blessing that they have in Christ. The second prayer is that they will claim these blessings and utilize these blessings. It is one thing to have knowledge, and an entirely different thing to apply that knowledge to everyday life.

I can get a notice from the post office that I have an important package waiting for me. The package is mine. It is there at the post office with my name on it. No one else can have it. But what good does that package do me if I never go and claim it?

Or I could have a million dollars in the bank. But what good does a million dollars do me if I never write checks on it and put that money to good use?

Many people attend church and know Christian doctrine and theology, yet they do not daily live out these truths. They may even memorize Scripture, but they never live out what the Scriptures say. So they live in spiritual poverty. Here, Paul prays that we will not only know God's truth, but that we will live according to his truth. He prays that we will not only know that God has blessed us in Christ with every spiritual blessing in the heavenly places, but that we will put our blessings to good use. He writes:

> For this reason I bow my knees before the Father, from whom every family in heaven and on earth is named, that according to the riches of his glory he may grant you to be strengthened with power through his Spirit in your inner being, so that Christ may dwell in your hearts through faith—that you, being rooted and grounded in love, may have strength to comprehend with all the saints what is the breadth and length and height and depth, and to know the love of Christ that surpasses knowledge, that you may be filled with all the fullness of God (3:14-19).

Paul writes, "*For this reason* I bow my knees before the Father..." For what reason? For the reason that the Gentiles and the Jews have become one body in Christ. The phrase "from whom every family in heaven and on earth is named" refers to the fact that the saints of God from every age—those who are already in heaven and those who are still living on earth—derive their name from God the Father. They are one family because God is their Father.

It is commonly said in the secular world that we are all God's children, and God is the Father of everyone. No, he's not! God is the Creator of everyone, but only those who take Jesus as their Savior and Lord can claim God as their Father.

Paul goes on to pray "that according to the riches of his glory he may grant you to be strengthened with power through his Spirit in your inner being" (3:16). The way we know whether we are appropriating the Spirit's power in our lives is if we are growing spiritually. If, spiritually speaking, we are at the same place now that we were ten years ago, then we are not appropriating the power of the Holy Spirit in our lives.

How do we appropriate the power of the Holy Spirit? The old country preacher explained it best: "After you come to Christ, there are two tigers living inside of you. The one you feed the most will grow big and powerful. And the one you starve will die a slow death." As we feed regularly upon the Word of God, we grow in faith, godliness, and good works. And while we grow spiritually, our sin nature starves, becomes stunted, and dies a slow death. So to appropriate and utilize every blessing God has given us, we must starve sin and feed our new nature in Christ every day.

Letting Jesus love others through us

In my early Christian life, I was young and immature. But I also knew that God was calling me to preach and proclaim his Word. I remember one time crying to God in prayer, "Lord, please get somebody else to do this. I'm short-tempered, critical, and judgmental. I'm harsh and cutting. And I just do not see how you could use me."

The Lord answered my prayer—not by getting someone else to do it but by working on my character flaws. He said, "Don't worry. I'll help you take care of defects in your character." And ever since that time, all of these sins have been dying a slow death. I wish they'd die faster. I wish I could tell you that they are dead and buried. But they are dying nonetheless.

Paul goes on to tell us in verses 17-18, "so that Christ may dwell in your hearts through faith—that you, being rooted and grounded in love, may have strength to comprehend with all the saints what is the breadth and length and height and depth..."

Why does Paul have to pray that Christ may dwell in our hearts? Aren't all believers indwelt by the Holy Spirit? Yes, we are. Yet the daily process of becoming more like Christ—a process called sanctification—is a long process. We must die to self daily in order to live for Christ.

Whenever the president of the United States goes anywhere, an advance team goes ahead of him to prepare everything for his arrival. They stay with him and make sure that everything goes according to plan until he leaves. The Holy Spirit of God is the "advance team" of the Lord Jesus. The Spirit prepares our hearts for Christ's indwelling.

When the Lord Jesus Christ comes to dwell in us, he does not come as a guest or a temporary tenant. He comes to take ownership. The more areas of our lives we surrender to the Lord's control, the more indwelling of Christ we have in our lives.

The primary evidence of the Lord's indwelling in our lives is love. Paul prays in verses 18 and 19 that believers "may have strength to comprehend with all the saints what is the breadth and length and height and depth, and to know the love of Christ that surpasses knowledge, that you may be filled with all the fullness of God." The more room we give Christ in our lives, the more he reveals to us his incomprehensible love. The more we welcome him, the more love we experience.

The more he exercises lordship over our lives, the more he displays his love in us and through us.

Some Christians grit their teeth and say to themselves, *I've got to have more loving feelings for others*. But Christlike love is not an emotion or a warm, fuzzy feeling toward others. When Jesus said, "Love your enemies," he wasn't saying we should have warm, fuzzy feelings toward people who hate us and hurt us. There's nothing wrong with warm, fuzzy feelings, but that is not the kind of love the Bible talks about.

Genuine Christian love is an attitude of selflessness. Love is an act of the will to do good toward everyone, including those who hate us and hurt us. We may not feel loving toward everyone, but we can treat everyone in a loving way, regardless of our emotions.

When we give the Lord Jesus Christ more and more room in our lives, we cannot help but become more loving because Jesus will love others through us. When we become rooted and grounded in love, we will begin to comprehend the vastness of the love of God, the completeness of the love of God, and the totality of the love of God. That's what Paul means by the "breadth and length and height and depth" of God's love.

As we learn to love others with the love of Christ, we discover that God loves people we could never love in our own strength—and we begin to see how God has unconditionally loved us in spite of our own unloveliness and unlovableness. We begin to understand that his love lasts for all eternity. His love plunges to the depths of our humanity, reaching to the lowest and most degrading of sins. His love reaches to the heights of glory, lifting us up and exalting his own to the highest heaven.

And as we come to know the love of Christ that surpasses knowledge, we find that we become "filled with all the fullness of God." The more of ourselves we give over to his love and his control, the more he occupies us and fills us. His presence and his joy fills us to overflowing. It floods our hearts, minds, emotions, and intellect until our joy, our excitement, and our exuberant Christian love overflows to others.

Far more than we ask

Paul concludes his prayer with these exultant words in the final two verses of Ephesians 3:

> Now to him who is able to do far more abundantly than all that we ask or think, according to the power at work within us, to him be glory in the church and in Christ Jesus throughout all generations, forever and ever. Amen (3:20-21).

God is able to do far more than we ask of him when we truly yield all that we are and all that we have to him. There is no way this side of heaven that we can fully comprehend these truths. That is why we need God's perspective on life today—and why we will spend all of eternity comprehending and praising the incredible love of God.

5

The Unity of the Spirit

Ephesians 4:1-6

I once had dinner with two prominent evangelical leaders in England. Our host asked me to give thanks for the food, and I began by saying, "Lord, your Word said, 'How beautiful it is when the brethren dwell together...'"

One of the two men interrupted my prayer and added a phrase I had omitted: "in unity." This man was correct. That is the complete text. I was a little flustered, but I repeated the words, "in unity," and continued the prayer.

I was irritated—not with this Christian brother who had corrected me, but with myself for misquoting the verse by omitting that all-important phrase. Afterward, as I pondered my error, I realized that the phrase "in unity" is vitally important to the meaning of that verse. Any two roommates can dwell together in the same apartment, but they may not be in unity. A husband and wife can dwell together under one roof, but they may not be in unity. And any two church members can sit side by side in the same pew, but they may not be in unity.

The verse I quoted (or misquoted), Psalm 133:1, reads this way in the English Standard Version:

> Behold, how good and pleasant it is
> when brothers dwell in unity!

This verse speaks of a blessing—an experience of goodness and pleasant feelings—when brothers dwell in unity. But the blessing flows not from the dwelling together, but from the unity! This concept of unity among believers is one of the central concepts of the Christian life.

Jesus, in Matthew 18:19, promised that when two agree together there is a blessing in answer to prayer. And in John 17, in the high priestly prayer of Jesus before he went to the cross, the Lord prayed that the disciples would be united so they would be blessed and the world would come to know him through their unity.

The apostle Peter, in 1 Peter 3:7, wrote that when a husband and wife are together in unity there is a blessing in answer to their prayer. And in at least five places in the book of Acts, we see that when the early Christians prayed together in one accord, miracles happened and their prayers were answered.

God is always present in a special way through our unity. When Christians are in agreement and loving harmony, God is able to bless them and bring glory to his name.

What is Christian unity? Does it mean that we should all look alike, sound alike, and think alike? No. In fact, we often experience the height of Christian unity amid differences of opinion and differing ideas. The reality of Christian unity takes us far deeper than whether or not we agree on certain issues. Christians can and must be unified, accepting one another, loving one another, and forgiving one another in spite of their disagreements.

Paul answers all of our questions about Christian unity in Ephesians 4. And he answers with one all-important word: "Spirit."

The unity of the Spirit

Paul gives us a simple yet masterful explanation of how we are to maintain Christian unity in the first six verses of Ephesians 4:

> I therefore, a prisoner for the Lord, urge you to walk in a manner worthy of the calling to which you have been called, with all humility and gentleness, with patience, bearing with one another in love, eager to maintain the unity of the Spirit in the bond of peace. There is one body and one Spirit—just as you were called to the one hope that belongs to your call—one Lord, one faith, one baptism, one God and Father of all, who is over all and through all and in all (4:1-6).

What if Paul's only statement on Christian unity had been verse 3: "maintain the unity of the Spirit in the bond of peace"? We would not have any idea how to carry out that command. There would be hundreds of theories as to how a Christian should maintain the unity of the Spirit in the Christian church.

But Paul's counsel in verses 1 through 5 is clear, practical, and unambiguous. He sandwiches verse 3 between two bookends that tell us exactly how we are to maintain Christian unity in the bond of peace. In the first bookend, verses 1 and 2, he gives us four ingredients for producing the unity of the Spirit: "I therefore, a prisoner for the Lord, urge you to walk in a manner worthy of the calling to which you have been called, with all humility and gentleness, with patience, bearing with one another in love."

The four ingredients in the first bookend are aspects of spiritual maturity: humility, gentleness, patience, and forbearing love. If we make a lifelong habit of practicing and growing stronger in these four character traits, we are going to naturally maintain the unity of the Spirit in the bond of peace. We are going to bring reconciliation out of division, harmony out of strife, and trust out of an atmosphere of suspicion.

The second bookend is found in verses 4 through 6, in which Paul gives us seven reasons or rationales for maintaining the unity of the Spirit: "There is one body and one Spirit—just as you were called to the one hope that belongs to your call—one Lord, one faith, one baptism, one God and Father of all, who is over all and through all and in all."

If we continually meditate on the fact that we have one body (the church), one Spirit who indwells every member of that body, one hope of salvation, one Lord who died for us, one faith, one baptism, and one God the Father who is supreme over everything—then we will be motivated and convicted to maintain our unity with our fellow Christians.

The world is divided. America is divided. Homes and families are divided. And yes, many churches are divided. We are divided because we have allowed selfishness, ambition, impatience, bitterness, and hostility to reign in our lives instead of humility, gentleness, patience, and forbearing love. We are divided because we forget that we are all one body, filled with one Spirit, focused on one hope, worshipping one Lord, believing one faith, baptized into one baptism, and serving one God the Father.

We fall into the mind-set of thinking that everything is about *me*. We ask, "What about *my* feelings? What about *my* rights? What about what *I* want?" When the self is at the center of our thinking, unity collapses. Peace is destroyed. Conflict and division reign.

Notice how Paul opens Ephesians 4: "I therefore, a prisoner for the Lord, urge you to walk in a manner worthy of the calling to which you have been called." He reminds the believers that he is a prisoner. It's as if he is saying, "If you are quarreling with other Christians over your own ego, your own feelings, your own rights, your own preferences, consider this: I am a prisoner for the Lord. I have surrendered my ego, my feelings, my rights, and my very freedom for the sake of serving Christ."

When Paul calls himself "a prisoner for the Lord," he makes it clear that he does not view himself as a prisoner of the Roman government, even though he was in a Roman prison cell. And he doesn't view himself a prisoner of the Jewish religious leaders who brought false accusations against him. In Paul's mind, he was a prisoner of the Lord Jesus Christ.

That's why Paul did not feel sorry for himself. When he called himself "a prisoner for the Lord," he was not looking for sympathy. He was saying, "Let me be your example. As a prisoner for the Lord, I am not focused on my own convenience, my own rights, my own feelings, my own preferences. I am honored merely to be a prisoner for the Lord. As his prisoner, I urge you to follow my example and live a life of humility, gentleness, patience, and forbearing love. Do this—and you will maintain the unity of the Spirit in the bond of peace."

Paul's message of unity is as desperately important today in the twenty-first century as it was in the first century. If we want to fulfill the Lord's command to maintain unity in the church and peace in our relationships, we need to continually ask ourselves: Does my behavior benefit the work of God? Do my words bless the kingdom of God? Does the example of my life bring honor and praise to God? If we would ask ourselves these questions daily, even hourly, we would truly begin to live worthy of the calling to which we have been called.

When Paul says we should "walk in a manner worthy of the calling to which [we] have been called" (4:1), he is talking about balance. The word *worthy* in the original Greek suggests a balancing of the scales. If, on one side of the scale, we have Jesus Christ and all the mercy and blessings he has shown us, then on the other side of the scale there ought to be a balancing amount of gratitude, which we display by living in a manner that is honoring and pleasing to the Lord.

On one side of the scale is the One who saved us, redeemed us, called us, chose us, predestined us, and adopted us. On the other side of the scale is our obedience, which proceeds from a heart that overflows with thankfulness to him. When we are living in total obedience and gratitude toward God, unity and peace will permeate our lives.

The four virtues of unity and peace

Let's take a closer look at the four virtues that Paul says will produce a lifestyle of unity and peace (4:2). These four virtues are the practical means by which we walk worthy of our calling in Christ.

1. Humility. A humble spirit is absolutely vital to maintaining unity and peace in any church or family. The opposite of humility is pride. When pride sets in there is nothing but war and conflict. Pride, in fact, is the sin that caused the fall of Satan (see Ezekiel 28:12-19 and 1 Timothy 3:6).

How can a husband and wife experience unity and peace when each claims to be right all the time? Neither will ever admit fault or confess to being wrong. Pride has driven a wedge into their relationship.

How can a church or any other group of believers maintain the unity of the Spirit when each person is in love with his or her own brilliance, ideas, and points of view? Their selfish pride will produce nothing but conflict. As Paul wrote to the Romans:

> Love one another with brotherly affection. Outdo one another in showing honor...Live in harmony with one another. Do not be haughty, but associate with the lowly. Never be wise in your own sight (Romans 12:10,16).

It is said that when thoroughbred horses are attacked by an outside enemy, they stand in a circle, face each other, and kick the enemy with their hind legs. Donkeys, it is said, do the opposite. They circle up and face the enemy, then use their hind legs to kick each other. That is an example of how stubborn, donkey-like pride can destroy our relationships and our unity. When pride sets in, we ignore the real enemy and start kicking each other.

It's clear that our culture glorifies prideful people, but the glorification of pride is not a modern invention. The ancient Greeks considered pride to be a virtue, and they didn't even have a word for humility. Christians in the first century were forced to coin a word to describe what God did in Christ. The Greek language simply lacked the words to describe the humility that drove the Creator of the universe to leave his home in glory to be born in a manger and live in utter poverty. Jesus owned nothing but his clothes. He had nowhere to lay his head. He died a criminal's death and was buried in a borrowed tomb. There was no Greek word to describe that kind of humility.

But God, through Paul, tells us that humility is the very first secret to maintaining unity and peace in a Christian family or in a Christian church.

2. Gentleness. A gentle spirit is essential to maintaining the unity of the Spirit. Another English word often used to express a gentleness of spirit is *meekness*. Many people, when they hear the word *meekness*, think of weakness. But the Bible teaches that meekness or gentleness is actually a character strength and a spiritual virtue.

The word *meekness* is borrowed from the profession of taming wild animals, especially horses. A tamed (or meek) horse is still every bit as strong as a wild horse. Gentle horses do not lose their strength by being tamed. In fact, the very act of taming a horse enables us to control, channel, and discipline its strength so that the horse's strength can be put to effective use.

Gentleness is when you have the power to take revenge—but you choose to forgive and show love instead. Gentleness is when you have the power to strike back—but you choose to heal instead. Gentleness is when you have the power to destroy—but you use that power to build up and edify instead.

The meek and gentle Christian who practices restraint, who freely dispenses grace and forgiveness, and who channels his or her power for good is a Christian who is well equipped to maintain the unity of the Spirit in the bond of peace.

3. Patience. A patient person is one who doesn't quit, who doesn't give up on God's promises. Abraham waited patiently for 25 years for God to fulfill his promise. Noah waited patiently for 120 years before he saw a drop of rain and the fulfillment of God's promise. Jeremiah was told to minister to people who would not believe his message; they insulted him, mocked him, and reviled him. But he patiently ministered nonetheless.

The apostle Paul patiently endured all sorts of hardships—beatings, floggings, stonings, shipwrecks, persecution, slander, attacks from false Christians, hunger, thirst, and more (see 2 Corinthians 11:24-27). No question, Paul was a patient, persevering man! He never gave up on God's promises, never stopped trusting in God's protection, and never considered God to be unfair or unkind in allowing him to go through trials and danger for the cause of Christ.

If we are patient in our dealings with our fellow Christians and family members, including our dealings with difficult people, God will use us. We will become instruments of God's peace, maintaining the unity of the Spirit.

4. Forbearing love. There are different Greek words for love. *Eros* is a selfish love that refers to an appreciation of beauty, pleasure, and sensual experiences. It is not a giving love but a love that takes. *Storge* is familial love—for example, the natural, cherishing affection of a parent for a child or a child for a parent. *Phileo* is the reciprocal love and fondness between friends—a love that gives as long as it receives. But Christlike *agape*—the word for love that Paul uses here—is a love that is totally unselfish. It is the love that gives and asks for nothing in return.

Selfless, forbearing, Christlike *agape-love* is the umbrella trait that encompasses all other virtues. If you truly love God and love others, you will be humble, gentle, patient, and forbearing with everyone around you. If you practice these four virtues day in and day out, especially in those tough times when you are mistreated, and if you do so prayerfully and in reliance on the power of the Holy Spirit, you will become a powerful force for maintaining the unity of the Spirit in the bond of peace, regardless of your circumstances.

Understand that this is not a guarantee that you can avoid all conflict. There are always some people who are hostile and difficult, no matter how humbly you speak, how gently you treat them, how patient you are with them, and how selflessly you love them. That's why Paul writes to the Christians in Rome, "If possible, so far as it depends on you, live peaceably with all" (Romans 12:18). You can't control anyone else's behavior or attitude; but as far as it depends on you, these four virtues can make you an agent of peace in your family and your church.

One God, one faith, one hope

In Paul's second bookend, he gives us seven reasons or rationales for maintaining the unity of the Spirit:

> There is one body and one Spirit—just as you were called to the one hope that belongs to your call—one Lord, one faith, one baptism, one God and Father of all, who is over all and through all and in all (4:4-6).

Unity is the very essence of our faith. Our God is one. Our faith is one. Our baptism is one. Our hope is one. Our spiritual family is one. So whenever we do anything that causes division, separation, or factions within the church, we violate the essence of our faith.

Christians are not like the Hindus, who have twenty-three million gods. We have one God. He is the triune God, but he is one God, not three gods. The three persons in the Godhead are in perfect unity all the time. Each person of the Trinity has a unique role, yet there is not the slightest hint of conflict within the Godhead.

We don't have two billion holy spirits indwelling each believer. There is one Holy Spirit who indwells us all. He indwells me and he indwells you if you are a worshipper of Jesus Christ. That one Spirit is the unifying life-force within the body of Christ.

When Paul says there is only one faith, he is talking about the set of doctrines and beliefs by which we live, day by day. He is talking about our one and only gospel, our one and only way to salvation, and our one and only way to heaven. People today have largely bought into the lie that there are many roads, many spiritual paths, but they all lead to the same God and the same heaven. But the Bible teaches clearly that there is one way, and it is a narrow way.

There is only one baptism by which we identify with Christ. Many people don't understand that the root meaning of the word *baptism* is "to identify with." In the early church, when Christians were baptized by the Holy Spirit after they came to Christ, they stepped into the waters of baptism for one reason and one reason only—to publicly identify themselves with Christ. To publicly identify with Christ through baptism was often punishable by death in the ancient world, and it is still punishable by death in many parts of the world today.

We have one hope, not dozens or hundreds of hopes. All who are in Christ Jesus are going to the same heaven where Jesus is, whether we go there in death or we remain until the Lord returns. There is only one hope of heaven. Of that, we can be sure.

We have one Christian family—the church. We speak many languages in this family. Some baptize by sprinkling, others baptize by immersion. Some have loud, rowdy, shouting worship celebrations while others worship according to a traditional, formal liturgy. Some serve grape juice in the communion cup; others serve fermented wine. These are all matters of form, not substance. They make no difference. We are all one family.

In heaven, we will all be one with Christ. We will see our heavenly Father and our Lord Jesus Christ—and our unity in the Spirit will be complete at last.

6

The Gifts of the Spirit

Ephesians 4:7-16

Suppose you offered me a gift—and I *refused* it. What would you think of me? Would you think I was prideful and ungrateful?

Or suppose you offered me a gift—and I took that gift, set it on a shelf, and never even bothered to unwrap it? What would you think of me? Would you think I was careless and thoughtless?

Or suppose you offered me a gift—and I tossed the gift in the trash? What would you think of me? Would you think I was rude and inconsiderate?

If that is how I treated your gift, would you feel hurt? Disappointed? Brokenhearted? You might say, "It's inconceivable that anyone would ever treat a gift—and the giver of that gift—in such a thoughtless, hurtful way!"

Yet that is exactly how many Christians treat the gifts the Lord Jesus Christ has given them. After his resurrection, after he ascended into heaven, Jesus gave gifts to each of his children. As Paul writes in Ephesians:

> But grace was given to each one of us according to the measure of Christ's gift. Therefore it says,
> "When he ascended on high he led a host of captives,
> and he gave gifts to men" (4:7-8).

The Lord gave at least one gift to every one of his children. Every time someone comes to Christ and is born of the Spirit of God, God gives that person a "spiritual birthday gift."

And it's not just any old randomly selected gift, purchased at a bargain basement at giveaway prices. This gift was custom-selected to match the believer's personality and uniqueness. God lavished infinite care and consideration on the selection of this gift, and it is measured and tailor-made to the individual's specific capabilities.

But how do we, his children, treat the gifts he has given us? And how does God feel when we reject or set aside the gifts he has given us?

The one and only irreplaceable you

God's gifts to us are a serious matter—so serious and important that God inspired the apostle Paul to emphasize spiritual gifts at least three times. Paul writes about spiritual gifts in Ephesians 4, Romans 12, and 1 Corinthians 12.

If you combine all of Paul's three lists of spiritual gifts, you couldn't possibly exhaust the variety of gifts. For example, there is not just one kind of teaching gift; there are many different and varied teaching gifts. You can find a hundred believers with a teaching gift, yet no two of them are alike. They differ from one another in emphasis, ability, style, and area of expertise. Some excel in teaching adults, others in teaching children or adolescents. Some are great mentors and one-on-one teachers, while others are more effective when teaching large groups of people. They are as different from each other as snowflakes or fingerprints or strands of DNA.

Jesus purposely tailor-made a gift just for you. He took into account your personality, intellect, temperament, education, life experiences, and the needs of the people all around you. He has given each person more than one gift with endless varieties of combinations. God did not create us as human beings on an assembly line or stamp us out with cookie cutters—and that means that in God's sovereign plan, every Christian is irreplaceable. I can't replace you, and you can't replace me. If you don't use the gifts God has given you, God can't simply send someone else to take your place. If you do not fill the role God has given you, then the task God has assigned you won't get done.

When we refuse to accept our gifts, or we refuse to unwrap our gifts, or we simply despise and ignore the gifts Jesus has given us, we break the heart of the Giver, and we do harm to the body of Christ, his church. God placed us in the body for the edification and equipping of the body and for our growth. He gave us gifts in order to bless the work of Christ in the body.

A healthy body needs exercise, and that principle is as true for the body of Christ as for any physical body. If the body of Christ does not have everyone exercising his or her spiritual birthday gift, it is an unhealthy body. When we pretend that our gifts don't matter, when even one believer does not rightly minister his or her gift as God's steward, God's work is hindered. The church of Jesus Christ is in the mess it's in today because we have thousands of believers who are mere spectators in the body, not functioning limbs, muscles, and organs of the body.

You have a ministry to the body that nobody else can perform. You have a gift that nobody else can exercise. You have a contribution to make that nobody else can make. What are you going to do with the spiritual gifts God has given you?

The spoils of victory

Next, Paul quotes a prophecy about the Lord Jesus Christ that originally comes from Psalm 68:

> Therefore it says,
> "When he ascended on high he led a host of
> captives,
> and he gave gifts to men."
> (In saying, "He ascended," what does it mean but that he had also descended into the lower regions, the earth? He who descended is the one who also ascended far above all the heavens, that he might fill all things.) (4:8-10).

The image suggested here is that of a king who went out to the battlefield. There he valiantly fought the enemy and won a spectacular victory. Like all victorious kings in the days of King David, this king brought back home all the spoils of victory. He led a procession of "a host of captives." These captives were the officers and soldiers who had been taken prisoner in previous battles by the enemy. In defeating the enemy on the battlefield, this victorious king was able to set those captives free and lead them back home.

He also brought the trophies of his victory with him and paraded them for everyone to see—valuable items of gold and silver plundered from the enemy nation. Out of this plunder, the victorious king would give gifts to all his brave and victorious soldiers. He would distribute among his soldiers the spoils of victory as a reward for their glorious service.

Ever since the fall of Adam, Satan has held all of humanity captive. He has kept us all in his slave camps. We have been bound in chains of sin, forced to serve Satan, forced to labor for him as slaves.

But on the cross, King Jesus fought a fierce battle, defeating Satan, conquering sin and death. Through his resurrection and ascension, our victorious King Jesus took all the spoils from Satan. He wrested the title deed of planet Earth from Satan's hand—the deed Satan seized from Adam in the Garden of Eden. Our victorious King Jesus set his captured soldiers free from their chains. He set the captives free.

Then our victorious King Jesus divided the spoils and gave each of his children a special gift. That gift has each believer's name written on it. Your gift is only for you. He gave it to you on your spiritual birthday. Our triumphant, conquering Jesus distributed the spoils to all of his subjects. Not one was left out or passed over.

And it is a supremely precious gift. To purchase your gift, King Jesus paid the ultimate price on the cross.

> And he gave the apostles, the prophets, the evangelists, the pastors and teachers, to equip the saints for the work of ministry, for building up the body of Christ, until we all attain to the unity of the faith and of the knowledge of the Son of God, to mature manhood, to the measure of the stature of the fullness of Christ (4:11-13).

Purposeful gifts

Jesus came all the way to earth from the highest heaven so that you may have a spiritual gift. Are you beginning to understand the depth of his pain and grief when you say to him, "What gift? I don't have a gift. I'm too busy to bother myself with spiritual gifts."

But when we receive our gift gratefully and exercise it obediently, God is able to use our gift to bless others, to bless the church, and to carry out his eternal plan here on earth. It's the same principle as tithing. When we give God the first 10 percent of our earnings, the firstfruits of our labor, God not only puts that 10 percent to good use, but he also blesses and multiplies the other 90 percent. He enlarges and stretches it to bless us and to meet all our needs and wants.

In the same way, when we put the Lord first in everything—in our time, energy, and in our use of our tailor-made gifts—he will bless us. He will multiply our time. He will multiply our efforts and abilities. He will overwhelm us with blessings that are exceedingly, abundantly beyond what we can think or imagine.

In Ephesians 4, Paul limits his discussion of spiritual gifts to the leadership gifts. He elaborates on all of the gifts in Romans and 1 Corinthians, but the implication is that these are applicable to all of us. As you read through these passages, you come away with a list of gifts that includes the gifts of an apostle, evangelist, and pastor; gifts of prophecy, teaching, exhortation, giving, leadership, administration, mercy, service, discernment, faith, healing, helping, knowledge, wisdom, tongues, interpretation, and miracles. Some of us will have exceptional gifts in certain areas, yet we all have most of these gifts to some degree.

For example, you may know a fellow Christian with an extraordinary gift of evangelism—yet we are all called to be witnesses and evangelists, sharing the good news with the people around us. You may know a fellow Christian who has a powerful, exceptional gift of mercy—yet we are all commanded to be merciful in our dealings with others. Some Christians have an amazing gift of prophecy, the ability to apply God's Word to specific situations—yet God expects all of us as Christians to be able to open the Scriptures to family members or neighbors or friends and say, "Thus says the Lord."

You may not think you have the spiritual gift of a pastor, but doesn't God expect you to be a shepherd to your family? You may not think you have a special gift to be an apostle in the biblical sense, but aren't we all supposed to be God's "sent ones" (the literal meaning of *apostle*) wherever we go?

God has given us all many spiritual gifts, not just one or two. When we use our gifts as God intended, we not only please God, but we fulfill his sovereign plan by blessing his church and his work and by reaching the lost with his good news.

Could God carry out his plan by some other means? Of course. But in his sovereign will, he said, in effect, "I gave each of you these gifts to reach the lost and equip the saints." That is why, when he ascended on high, he gave us gifts.

He gave us spiritual gifts to equip us. The word *equip* is borrowed from the medical field. It was used when an orthopedist would set a bone that was broken. It was used to mean "help make whole." People all around us are desperate to be made whole. So our spiritual gifts equip us to be whole and to take the gospel of wholeness to a broken world.

Second, God gave us spiritual gifts for the work of service—service to God, service to the church, and service to individuals. Our gifts are not intended to enlarge our egos. They are gifts to be used in humble and committed Christian service.

Third, God gave us spiritual gifts to edify (build up) others. We are to spiritually edify one another, encourage one another, and lift up one another with our gifts. In order to use our gifts to edify others, we must be involved in the life of the church and in the lives of others.

Running after every religious circus

And there is yet another reason God gave us spiritual gifts, and that reason is found in the next verse:

> so that we may no longer be children, tossed to and fro by the waves and carried about by every wind of doctrine, by human cunning, by craftiness in deceitful schemes (4:14).

One of the key reasons God gave us spiritual gifts is so that his children would not remain immature in the faith. There is nothing more heartbreaking than to see an adult behaving like a child. It breaks God's heart when his children look for fulfillment everywhere except in him.

When I was a boy, the circus would come to town, and I would follow the circus parade all the way to the end. The next time another circus came to town, I was right there in that parade. That's what children do. But if you were to see a man in his fifties running after every circus that comes to town, you'd think there was something seriously wrong with that man. He lacks discernment and maturity. Ephesians 4:14 says that when we exercise our spiritual gifts, we become mature, no longer running after every religious circus that comes to town.

Some Christians run from seminar to seminar, teacher to teacher, and movement to movement, looking for the latest thing to promise spiritual fulfillment. The Word of God says that instead of chasing after the latest thing, we should grow deep and mature in Christlikeness as we discover and use our spiritual gifts. The immature Christian asks, "What can I get from God?" The mature Christian asks, "How can I use my spiritual gifts to serve other Christians and edify the body?" As Paul goes on to write:

> Rather, speaking the truth in love, we are to grow up in every way into him who is the head, into Christ, from whom the whole body, joined and held together by every joint with which it is equipped, when each part is working properly, makes the body grow so that it builds itself up in love (4:15-16).

Christians who neglect their spiritual gifts produce paralysis in the body of Christ, hampering its effectiveness and crippling its progress. But Christians who discover and use their spiritual gifts as God intended help to grow and complete the body of Christ, building up God's people in Christian love.

7

The Old Life and the New

Ephesians 4:17-32

If you feel angry when you hear people in our culture call good "evil" and evil "good," you're not alone. If you feel angry when you see the Christian faith attacked and distorted in the media, you're in good company. If you feel angry when you see people in our society lying to our young people about moral and spiritual virtues and manipulating their young minds, you're in good company.

In fact, if you never experience righteous anger, you should ask yourself why you are not emotionally involved in the moral and spiritual warfare going on all around you. It was righteous, godly anger, rightly channeled, that accomplished great reforms in our history, from the abolition of slavery to education reform to child-labor reform to civil rights reform.

For years I avoided making media appearances. I had heard the Scriptures distorted so often in the media that I simply wanted no part of it. The distortion of God's truth by many media preachers made me angry. But God dragged me into the world of radio and television, and I ultimately made my peace with the media. While many in the secular media present Christianity as a religion of hate, we proclaim the message of God's love. I could choose to put my fist through the TV screen every time I see a false preacher spreading misinformation over the airwaves, but God has shown me a better way. Now I channel my righteous anger into preaching biblical truth through our Leading the Way media ministry.

There is sinful anger and there is righteous anger, and we need to know the difference. "Be angry and do not sin; do not let the sun go down on your anger," Paul writes in Ephesians 4:26. This is an exhortation we would all do well to study, understand, and take to heart.

Ephesians 4:17-32 presents a contrast between what a Christian is and what a Christian is not. This is an excellent passage to share with anyone who is confused about Christianity, because it clearly states the truth that the world needs to know about the Christian faith and biblical Christians.

The non-Christian life

Paul begins this section of Ephesians by showing us what the non-Christian life is like:

> Now this I say and testify in the Lord, that you must no longer walk as the Gentiles do, in the futility of their minds. They are darkened in their understanding, alienated from the life of God because of the ignorance that is in them, due to their hardness of heart. They have become callous and have given themselves up to sensuality, greedy to practice every kind of impurity (4:17-19).

Without the light of Christ, the human mind is dark because the eyes of human thinking are blind. And the reason the eyes of our thinking are blind is because the Christless mind has deliberately chosen to live contrary to God's original design for humanity.

The decision to live apart from God's plan is rarely a sudden decision. It takes place gradually. First, we take one baby step of questioning God's revealed Word. Then we take another step of rationalizing some habitual sin we refuse to give up. Then another step of subtle rebellion. And with each small step we take away from God, we become more and more insensitive to the conviction and calling of the Holy Spirit. Eventually, a day arrives when we have lost our sensitivity to God. We have no more feelings for him.

Few people become instant addicts. An addiction usually starts slowly, imperceptibly, one small step at a time. You click on a pornographic website, but you don't want to get hooked, and you promise yourself you won't try it again. The next time, you feel guilty going back on the promise you made to yourself. You feel dirty, ashamed, and do it in secret, knowing what you're doing is wrong. Gradually, the addiction takes over your life. You crave it, live for it, and think only about these sites. You begin practicing your once-hidden addiction right out in the open, losing all sense of shame. In the end, the addiction claims you as a victim.

Paul writes that the addiction to sin and rebellion follows a similar pattern—a three-step progression toward complete rebellion against God:

1. The sinner, at first, becomes intellectually futile. You can't reason with him. He becomes darkened in his spiritual understanding.

2. The sinner deliberately ignores the truth. All the preaching and teaching in the world will not help the person who simply refuses to listen. He is alienated from the life of God because of his willful state of ignorance.

3. Finally, the sinner becomes callous—that is, hardened. He gives himself up to sensuality and sin, choosing moral impurity over the pure truth of God. His sin addiction is complete, and there is almost nothing you can say or do to reach the hardened heart of such a person.

God designed us to live by his standards and principles. Once we begin to turn aside from his will for our lives, once we begin to rebel against him, we start down the road to self-destruction.

The Greek-born Roman essayist Plutarch wrote about a youth of the Greek city-state Sparta. This young man stole a fox and planned to eat it. But when the boy saw the man from whom he had stolen the fox, he tried to keep his theft a secret. He hid the fox inside his cloak—and the frightened fox began eating the boy's flesh, chewing through his skin and tearing at the boy's vital organs. But the boy refused to cry in pain or even flinch. The boy endured being gnawed by the fox until he finally pitched over onto the ground, dead. Even at the cost of his own life, even at the cost of so much pain and suffering, the boy refused to own up to his wrongdoing.

This is a vivid picture of unbelievers in our culture today. They are so determined to deny that they are sinners, so steadfast in refusing to repent and turn to God, that they allow the foxes of sin to eat away at them and tear them up inside. And as they die, society dies with them.

That is Paul's description of the non-Christian world.

The Christian life

When Jesus Christ comes into a person's life, he radically changes that person, as Paul explains in the next few verses:

> But that is not the way you learned Christ!—assuming that you have heard about him and were taught in him, as the truth is in Jesus, to put off your old self, which belongs to your former manner of life and is corrupt through deceitful desires, and to be renewed in the spirit of your minds, and to put on the new self, created after the likeness of God in true righteousness and holiness (4:20-24).

A Christian is not a person who never sins. A Christian is someone who freely acknowledges his own failure, fallenness, and sinfulness—

and lives by faith in reliance on the power of God. Because Christians acknowledge their sinfulness and powerlessness, God gives each Christian a new heart, a new mind, a new nature, and a new way of life. From that time forward, that Christian lives a life of repentance and renewal.

Picture a street person dressed in filthy rags. You can smell him a mile away. He sleeps in the gutter. One day, the king comes to this person and asks, "Are you ready for a new life?" When the man says that he's ready, the king takes him to the royal palace, takes off the man's filthy rags, and has his servants bathe the man and dress him in new clothes of the finest silk. Now the vagrant is no longer a vagrant! He has a new life and a new identity as a gentleman—if he chooses to keep it.

But in order to keep his new life and his new identity, he must make a daily choice to continue living as a gentleman. He needs to maintain the cleanliness and hygiene of a gentleman. He needs to continue dressing like a gentleman. He needs to change his way of thinking and behaving and speaking so that he demonstrates the manner of a gentleman. He needs to have a different purpose and outlook on life. He must be conscious of the man he was before the king took him in—and the difference in his life after the king changed his life.

He must remember that he was once a man of the gutter, but now he is a man of the palace. He once was a man of rags, but now he is a man of riches. If he forgets that he came from the gutter, he is in danger of going back to the gutter. Only by remembering where he came from, and remembering how the king transformed his life, can the man keep from sliding back into the old ways and returning to the gutter.

The analogy of the transformed street person illustrates a principle that Paul describes here in Ephesians 4. Paul does not claim that our Christian conversion, our radical spiritual transformation, should obliterate all memory of our previous life. In fact, like any vagrant, we will be tempted at times to go back to our old ways, our old life in the gutter. We may experience moments of "temporary spiritual insanity," thinking we miss the old life.

But if we remember our old life in the gutter and remember how our King Jesus transformed our lives by moving us into his palace, we will be able to resist the lure and temptation of the gutter. We may even slide back into the gutter from time to time—but we won't stay there. Once we have experienced the palace of King Jesus, so rich in love, forgiveness, blessing, and grace, the gutter will always seem strange and unpleasant to us. A genuine believer will never want to go back and live permanently in the gutter again.

The old life versus the new

The old life was corrupt. It led us to ruin and destruction. But the new life is as beautiful as creation itself. The old life was dominated by the uncontrolled, undisciplined pursuit of self-indulgent pleasure. The new life is holy and righteous and pure. It is still a life of pleasure, but the deep and lasting pleasures of the new life are rooted in a love of God and a love for others, not the vain indulgence of the self.

In the next few verses, Paul explains the new life in practical terms:

> Therefore, having put away falsehood, let each one of you speak the truth with his neighbor, for we are members one of another. Be angry and do not sin; do not let the sun go down on your anger, and give no opportunity to the devil. Let the thief no longer steal, but rather let him labor, doing honest work with his own hands, so that he may have something to share with anyone in need. Let no corrupting talk come out of your mouths, but only such as is good for building up, as fits the occasion, that it may give grace to those who hear. And do not grieve the Holy

> Spirit of God, by whom you were sealed for the day of redemption. Let all bitterness and wrath and anger and clamor and slander be put away from you, along with all malice. Be kind to one another, tenderhearted, forgiving one another, as God in Christ forgave you (4:25-32).

In this passage, Paul gives us five vivid before-and-after contrasts, five comparisons of life without Christ versus life with Christ:

First, life without Christ consists of perpetual lying, cheating, and destroying the reputation of others. It's a life of deception and falsehood. Paul writes, "Therefore, having put away falsehood, let each one of you speak the truth with his neighbor, for we are members one of another." We are to speak the truth in love.

Second, life without Christ is a life of uncontrollable anger, rage, resentment, and bitterness. It is a life of selfish hostility that lashes out whenever pride is injured. Paul writes, "Be angry and do not sin; do not let the sun go down on your anger, and give no opportunity to the devil."

Christians still feel angry, but their anger is kindled by the things that kindle the anger of God: sin and injustice. Those who live apart from Christ are easily angered on their own behalf. But when Christ is living in us and through us, we are no longer obsessed with our own pride. We may become angry on behalf of the weak and helpless who suffer injustice and persecution, but we are less likely to be angry on our own behalf. If we succumb to selfish anger, we know it's not natural or healthy, so we make a commitment to resolve our anger before sundown so that it doesn't harden into bitterness and resentment. Once we allow bitterness to take root in our lives, we leave the door open for the enemy to come in and wreak havoc in our lives and our relationships.

Third, life without Christ is a life of stealing, of taking what is not yours, of violating the rights of others and bringing harm to them. Before we say, "Well, I'm no thief; I would never steal," we need to remember that padding the expense account and cheating on our taxes and downloading pirated music or movies is stealing too. Paul writes, "Let the thief no longer steal, but rather let him labor, doing honest work with his own hands, so that he may have something to share with anyone in need."

Christians work hard and joyfully, faithfully giving *more* effort than their employers require. We earn our income in order to share generously with the needy. Life with Christ means that we are focused on giving, not getting.

Fourth, life without Christ is a life of cursing and abusive speech. The non-Christian world reeks of foul, coarse, offensive speech. But Paul writes, "Let no corrupting talk come out of your mouths, but only such as is good for building up, as fits the occasion, that it may give grace to those who hear." Life with Christ is a life of wholesome, encouraging words that build others up and never tear down.

Why is our speech so important? It's because, when we speak words that are more consistent with Satan's character than Christ's character, the Holy Spirit is grieved. Paul writes, "And do not grieve the Holy Spirit of God, by whom you were sealed for the day of redemption." The Holy Spirit dwells within us. The Spirit has a mind, a will, and feelings. The Spirit is our Comforter (see John 14:26). When you grieve the one who comforts you, where will you go for comfort?

Fifth, life without Christ is full of bitterness. Paul writes, "Let all bitterness and wrath and anger and clamor and slander be put away from you, along with all malice. Be kind to one another, tenderhearted, forgiving one another, as God in Christ forgave you."

Why do we see so much bitterness all around us? Why are our homes filled with bitterness? Why is there so much bitterness and resentment in our business relationships, our churches, and our neighborhoods? Why do we see so much bitterness in our political system, in our news and entertainment media, and on the Internet?

It's because bitterness, like a poisonous plant, has a way of burrowing underground and taking root in people's lives. That is why we read in the book of Hebrews, "See to it that no one fails to obtain the grace of God; that no 'root of bitterness' springs up and causes trouble, and by it many become defiled" (Hebrews 12:15). A root of bitterness symbolizes anger that festers, becoming foul and poisonous. Whenever we fail to completely forgive other people, whenever we secretly harbor a grudge against someone, we are allowing bitterness to put down roots into the depths of our lives.

How do you know if a root of bitterness has gone down deep into your life? Simply ask yourself: *Can I go to the person who has hurt me deeply and give that person a hug—and mean it?* If not, then you probably have work to do in forgiving that person.

A root of bitterness can choke the life out of your soul. It can strangle your joy and your love for others. Life with Christ is a life of forgiveness.

God did not hold a grudge against you and me. When we deserved all of his wrath, God showed kindness toward us. When we deserved judgment, he forgave us. While we were still sinning and rebelling against him, God sent his Son to die in our place. If God has done all of that for us, who are we to withhold forgiveness from those who have wronged us?

John Wesley said, "Give me one hundred men who fear nothing but sin and desire nothing but God, and I care not whether they be clergyman or laymen, they alone will shake the gates of Hell and set up the kingdom of Heaven upon the earth."[2]

Christian, go out and shake the gates of hell!

8

From Darkness to Light

Ephesians 5:1-17

Mr. Greene worked as a cab driver in San Antonio, Texas. One Christmas season, he heard that Christians in Henderson County had put up a nativity scene at the county courthouse in Athens, Texas. A strong advocate of "freedom from religion," Mr. Greene was incensed. He considered it unconstitutional for any religious symbol to be placed on government property.

Though Mr. Greene's income was modest and Athens was five hours from his home in San Antonio, he decided to scrape together his resources and file suit against Henderson County, demanding that the nativity scene be removed. He also planned to lead a protest rally at the courthouse.

Many Christians in Henderson Country reacted angrily. They wondered, *What right does this San Antonio atheist have to come here and ruin our Christmas tradition?*

Within days, however, Mr. Greene abruptly dropped his planned protest and withdrew the lawsuit. His reason: he had been diagnosed with a detached retina, and it appeared that he might be going blind. He quit his job as a taxi driver, fearing that if his eyesight failed suddenly, he would endanger his passengers. He had no health insurance and could not afford an operation to repair the retina.

When the Christians of Athens, Texas, heard of Mr. Greene's eyesight issues, there were two reactions. One group of Christians seemed to take a vindictive "serves him right" attitude. But others, led by Jessica Crye of San Springs Baptist Church, felt a Christlike compassion for the man who had tried to remove the nativity scene. Mrs. Crye and other Christians from the Athens community organized a fund-raiser to help Mr. Greene get treatment for his detached retina.

The fund-raiser produced four hundred dollars, plus an offer from several Henderson County believers to pay the entire bill for Mr. Greene's eye surgery. Mr. Greene accepted the money with surprise and gratitude, and he used it to buy groceries while he made arrangements to receive Social Security payments. But he refused the offer to pay his medical expenses because there was a good chance the surgery would not be successful, and he didn't want anyone to waste their money on his account.

Mr. Greene even took a portion of the donations he'd received and used it to purchase a lighted star for the Henderson County nativity scene. "I saw the nativity scene on a video on YouTube," Mr. Greene told a reporter. "There's no star on top of it. Shouldn't there be one?" He added that he hoped the Christians of Henderson County didn't mind that an atheist bought them a star.[3]

Since that time, Mr. Greene has announced that he has committed his life to Christ.

As Christians, we must always remember that we are role models. We represent the message and the character of the Lord Jesus Christ. We set an example to the world. When atheists attack believers, how should believers respond? By returning fire? By striking back? By saying, "Serves him right," when an atheist suffers misfortune? Or should we respond with Christlike, unconditional love and generosity?

The life-changing power of a Christian role model is staggering. Many people have been won to Christ without words. They have seen the life of Christ lived out in the quiet example of his people, and that was enough to persuade them to follow Christ. But many Christians, unfortunately, shrink from the responsibility that comes with being a role model of the Christian gospel.

As Christians, we are called to be Christlike examples to non-Christians. As Christian parents, we are called to set a Christlike example for our children. As Christian leaders, we should set a Christian example for our followers. As mature Christians, we are called to be role models of faith and character to younger Christians.

Jesus did not merely send us out to preach the gospel message. He called us to *follow him*—and that means we are to follow his example, not merely evangelizing with words, but becoming living role models of the gospel by living it out daily.

Imitators of God

We all learn from role models. The world's great artists all had role models, teachers, and mentors. They looked up to their role models and patterned their techniques after them. If you looked at a painting by Giovanni Bellini (1430–1516) and a painting by Vincent van Gogh (1853–1890), you would not see any similarity whatsoever in their styles and techniques. Yet there is an unbroken chain of influence from Bellini to van Gogh. Bellini strongly influenced his pupil Titian, who in turn was a major influence on Peter Paul Rubens. The paintings of Rubens heavily influenced Eugène Delacroix, and Delacroix was a major early influence on van Gogh.

Each of these painters developed a unique and individual approach to art, but all were influenced early in their careers by studying and imitating an artistic role model. This same principle is true in every endeavor, including the Christian life. That is why Paul wrote to the Corinthians, "Be imitators of me, as I am of Christ" (1 Corinthians 11:1). Like Paul, we should set a good example for other Christians to follow. And like Paul, we must remember that our ultimate role model is Jesus himself. In Ephesians, Paul writes:

> Therefore be imitators of God, as beloved children. And walk in love, as Christ loved us and gave himself up for us, a fragrant offering and sacrifice to God (5:1-2).

Paul invokes the image of God as our Father, and he encourages us to imitate our heavenly Father as a child imitates an earthly father. You have undoubtedly seen children imitating their father. You may have seen a little boy pounding a plastic peg into a plastic workbench with a plastic hammer, imitating the iron-and-lumber carpentry of his father. That is how we are to imitate God, our heavenly Father. We are to pattern ourselves after God as his dearly beloved children.

Paul does not ask us to imitate a God who is a taskmaster and slave driver, a terrifying and threatening tyrant, or a remote and unknowable deity in the clouds. We would not want to imitate such an image of God. No, he calls us to imitate God, our loving Father, who loves us as his children.

The word *imitate* in this verse literally means "to mimic." We are to play a game of "monkey-see, monkey-do" with God, doing everything we see him doing. If he loves, forgives, and shows grace to sinners, so should we. If he reaches out to the least, the last, and the lost, so should we. If he loves even those who curse him and hate him, so should we. Our challenge is to mimic God as perfectly as we are able, just as a child will mimic the words and actions of a parent.

A life of love

One of the central themes of Ephesians is that Christ's death and resurrection enable us to have access to the limitless riches and power of the Holy Spirit. God now permits us to enter his treasure house, and all the riches we see are ours through Christ. That is what the letter to the Ephesians is all about.

The foundation of our treasure house is Jesus. When Jesus is ours, everything that belongs to Jesus is ours too. His grace is ours. His mercy is ours. His love and forgiveness are ours. Because everything that belongs to Jesus is ours, it's natural that we should imitate him. We imitate him by extending his forgiving grace to others and by extending his love to others. That is why Paul writes, "And walk in love, as Christ loved us and gave himself up for us, a fragrant offering and sacrifice to God" (5:2).

This is the third time the apostle Paul hammers home the theme of Christlike love in this epistle. Paul understood human nature. He knew that our tendency is to love *only* those who love us. Our love is conditional. If you love me, I will love you; if you don't love me, I will punish you. We love those who reciprocate our love or those we think are worthy of our love. That's why Paul keeps telling us, in effect, "If you are going to be like God the Father, you must love others as God the Father loved you. To be like Christ, love as Christ loved you."

When I have performed weddings, I've made it clear to the couples that if they thought their marriage vows would keep them high on romantic love for the rest of their lives, they were sadly mistaken. I told them they could no more promise each other to be romantic all the time than they could promise never to get a headache. Romantic feelings ebb and flow, and sometimes they disappear.

But the loss of romantic love is *never* an excuse for dissolving a marriage. The love God commands a husband and wife to have for each other is not a feeling. It's a choice, a willful decision. Romantic love enhances and beautifies the marriage relationship, but the love God wants us to imitate is the Christlike love that is focused on giving, not getting. It is a love that is self-sacrificing, not self-centered.

Paul also warns us that, wherever real love is found, imitation love rears its ugly head. Whenever God establishes his love someplace, Satan shows up to offer his cheap counterfeit love.

How can you tell the difference between God's love and Satan's counterfeit? The contrast is clear: God's love is selfless, self-giving, and self-sacrificing. Satan's counterfeit love is selfish, self-indulgent, and self-serving. Most of the so-called love we see in the movies and on television is counterfeit, selfish love—the kind of "love" that leads to sexual immorality.

Counterfeit love destroys marriages and homes. Counterfeit love devastates the lives of children. Under the guise of so-called love, spouses walk out on families, leaving children with a hole in the soul that often never heals. People who follow counterfeit love are imitating Satan, not imitating God.

You might say, "My marriage is dead." Yet Jesus specializes in raising the dead, and he can raise your dead marriage. Those who have persevered through the ebb and flow of life and the loss of romantic love usually reach a point where they thank God for their perseverance. They have a greater bond and a stronger marriage than ever before.

Paul said that if you want to be imitators of God, don't give in to sexual immorality, which is a form of counterfeit love. He writes:

> But sexual immorality and all impurity or covetousness must not even be named among you, as is proper among saints. Let there be no filthiness nor foolish talk nor crude joking, which are out of place, but instead let there be thanksgiving. For you may be sure of this, that everyone who is sexually immoral or impure, or who is covetous (that is, an idolater), has no inheritance in the kingdom of Christ and God. Let no one deceive you with

> empty words, for because of these things the wrath of God comes upon the sons of disobedience. Therefore do not become partners with them (5:3-7).

Paul makes the case that when you love Christ, you want to imitate Christ. Therefore, you will be a model husband or wife, regardless of the ups and downs and the trials and temptations of marriage.

Note verse 6, where Paul writes, "Let no one deceive you with empty words, for because of these things the wrath of God comes upon the sons of disobedience." Why does Paul worry about the believers being deceived by empty words? Because Paul knew that false teachers would come on the scene. They would come as pastors and religious teachers, speaking from pulpits, drawing large crowds—but their message would be full of deception and immorality.

Today there are religious preachers, teachers, authors, and seminar leaders who claim that God doesn't really object to an immoral way of life. But the reality is this: God's wrath is coming against the world, against "the sons of disobedience," because of these false teachings and immoral acts. For the time being, God's grace and forgiveness are extended to everyone who will repent and turn to the Lord. But when the justice of God is revealed on the day of judgment, his justice will be plain for all to see.

Some Christians indulge in sexual immorality and say, "The grace of God will cover my sin." Please understand: *grace* is not synonymous with *license*. Grace is a gift, but it is also a responsibility. Grace is a privilege, but it is also an obligation. As Paul writes in his letter to the Christians in Rome:

> What shall we say then? Are we to continue in sin that grace may abound? By no means! How can we who died to sin still live in it? Do you not know that all of us who have been baptized into Christ Jesus were baptized into his death? We were buried therefore with him by baptism

> into death, in order that, just as Christ was raised from the dead by the glory of the Father, we too might walk in newness of life (Romans 6:1-4).

While God forgives everyone who repents, the Bible tells us that when you presume on the grace of God, it is an offense to the holy God. As imitators of God, we should love people as God loves people—and we must hate sin as God hates sin.

To be imitators of God, we must live in the light with God.

Darkness or light?

Before we belonged to Christ, we were darkness. Now we are light. In the next few verses, Paul contrasts the darkness and the light, and encourages us to live in the light:

> For at one time you were darkness, but now you are light in the Lord. Walk as children of light (for the fruit of light is found in all that is good and right and true), and try to discern what is pleasing to the Lord.
>
> Take no part in the unfruitful works of darkness, but instead expose them. For it is shameful even to speak of the things that they do in secret. But when anything is exposed by the light, it becomes visible, for anything that becomes visible is light. Therefore it says,
>
> "Awake, O sleeper,
> and arise from the dead,
> and Christ will shine on you."
>
> Look carefully then how you walk, not as unwise but as wise, making the best use of the time, because the days are evil. Therefore do not be foolish, but understand what the will of the Lord is (5:8-17).

Notice that Paul does not say, "We were living in the darkness and now we are living in the light." He says, "For at one time *you were darkness*, but now *you are light* in the Lord." When Jesus walked the earth, he was the light of the world. But he told his disciples that after he returned to the Father, *they would be light*. "You are the light of the world," he said. "A city set on a hill cannot be hidden" (Matthew 5:14).

If you are an imitator of God, you do not merely *reflect* his light—you *are* the light. How do you know that you are the light? You know you are the light if you are producing the deeds of light. Darkness hides ugly things, but light reveals them. Darkness does things in secret, but light operates in the open. Darkness produces concealment and subterfuge. Light is transparent and authentic.

In the Middle East, most of the street bazaars are held in narrow streets that are shaded by buildings and tent canopies. Before the advent of electricity, these bazaars were dark even in the middle of the day. So when people wanted to inspect the merchandise, they had to take the item out into the sunlight to make sure it had no flaws and that it was authentic.

Paul wants us to know that if we are sincerely imitating God, that is how we will live our lives—out in the open, in transparency and honesty. The person who lives his life in the shadows, hiding his actions and his true nature, is like someone in a deep sleep. That's why, in verse 14, he writes:

> "Awake, O sleeper,
> and arise from the dead,
> and Christ will shine on you."

Many Bible scholars and historians believe that these lines are from a hymn sung by the early church on Easter mornings.

"Look carefully then how you walk," Paul writes, "not as unwise but as wise." The psalmist tells us, "The fool says in his heart, 'There is no God'" (Psalm 14:1a). And Solomon reminds us, "The fear of the LORD is the beginning of wisdom, and the knowledge of the Holy One is insight" (Proverbs 9:10).

Wisdom is the application of God's Word to everyday situations. Some people confuse knowledge with wisdom, but they are not the same. Many people who have a great deal of knowledge have very little wisdom. And many people who lack worldly knowledge have a great deal of spiritual wisdom.

I once heard an estimate of the growth of human knowledge over the span of history. From the beginning of recorded history until 1845, the amount of knowledge accumulated by humankind was the equivalent of one inch. From 1845 to 1945, total human knowledge was equivalent to three inches. From 1945 to 1975, human knowledge expanded so rapidly that it was the equivalent of the height of the Washington Monument. From 1975 until 1995, human knowledge was equivalent to the height of the Empire State Building. Today, with the amount of information stored across the Internet, the amount of accumulated human knowledge is completely off any scale that makes sense to the human mind.

From the beginning of history until today, we have seen an absolutely staggering increase in human knowledge—but there has been no corresponding increase in wisdom. The world is still in darkness where wisdom is concerned. It truly seems that as knowledge expands, wisdom decreases.

You and I must plunge daily into God's Word and drink deeply of the wisdom that created the universe, and then we must walk wisely in that wisdom.

Paul concludes this section of Ephesians with a startling statement: "Look carefully then how you walk, not as unwise but as wise, making the best use of the time, because the days are evil. Therefore do not be foolish, but understand what the will of the Lord is."

The days are evil! We don't like to think that we live in evil days. We'd rather focus on building a comfortable life for ourselves, keeping up with friends on Facebook, watching our favorite TV shows (in high def and 3D), a weekly round of golf or a night out with friends, vacationing at the cabin or on the sailboat, saving up for a really great retirement—ah, the good life!

But Paul reminds us that the days are evil. Life is uncertain. The economy is unpredictable. An accident, a fire, a crime, a terminal diagnosis, a natural disaster, an economic meltdown—and the bottom could drop out of our safe, comfortable world at any moment. Make the best use of the time you have, Paul says, because the days are evil.

I meet people all the time who say, "I just want to enjoy life." Do you truly want to enjoy life? Good. If you want to make the most of the time and experience true joy, then turn off the TV and the computer, stop focusing on money and possessions, and reach beyond yourself. Start serving God and others.

The only true joy is found in serving people and telling them about the love of Jesus Christ. The very best way to use your time here on earth is by telling others how to experience eternity with Christ.

9

Spiritual Intoxication

Ephesians 5:18-20

We all know that alcoholism is a huge problem in our society. Even more distressing is the rise of alcoholism among teenagers. According to the U.S. Department of Health and Human Services, 20.7 million seventh through twelfth graders in America drink alcohol at least once a week.[4] More than 76 million Americans—about 43 percent of our adult population—have been exposed to, or must cope with, alcoholism in the family.[5] The economic cost of alcoholism has been estimated at well over $200 billion a year.[6] Drunk driving is responsible for the deaths of well over 10,000 people a year and injuring well over 200,000 a year. That is to say nothing of how many diseases are caused by alcoholism.[7]

People give all sorts of reasons and excuses for becoming intoxicated. Some say they like the feeling of loss of control. Others say they like to temporarily drown their sorrow and pain. But trying to escape into a bottle only makes problems grow worse. A member of Alcoholics Anonymous once wrote:

> We drank for happiness and became unhappy.
> We drank for joy and became miserable.
> We drank for sociability and became argumentative.
> We drank for sophistication and became obnoxious.
> We drank for friendship and made enemies.
> We drank for sleep and awakened without rest.
> We drank for strength and felt weak.
> We drank "medicinally" and acquired health problems.
> We drank for relaxation and got the shakes.
> We drank for bravery and became afraid.
> We drank for confidence and became doubtful.
> We drank to make conversation easier and slurred our speech.
> We drank to feel heavenly and ended up feeling like hell.
> We drank to forget and were forever haunted.
> We drank for freedom and became slaves.
> We drank to erase problems and saw them multiply.
> We drank to cope with life and invited death.[8]

A friend of mine, a recovering alcoholic, told me, "For years I believed the lie that I could not live without that drink. Once I realized it was a lie, God gave me victory."

Here in Ephesians 5, the apostle Paul contrasts the lie with the truth, the lure of alcohol intoxication versus the power that comes from being filled with the Holy Spirit. Paul writes:

> And do not get drunk with wine, for that is debauchery, but be filled with the Spirit, addressing one another in psalms and hymns and spiritual songs, singing and making melody to the Lord with your heart, giving thanks always and for everything to God the Father in the name of our Lord Jesus Christ (5:18-20).

The spirit of alcoholism, Paul writes, will depress you, but the Holy Spirit will elate you. The spirit of alcoholism will destroy your liver, but the Holy Spirit will strengthen your heart. The spirit of alcoholism will cost you a fortune, but the Holy Spirit will bring you blessings. The spirit of alcoholism will multiply your pain, but the Holy Spirit will heal you. The spirit of alcoholism will give you a hangover, but the Holy Spirit will comfort you. The spirit of alcoholism will temporarily deceive you into false happiness, but the Holy Spirit will give you true joy.

Earlier in Ephesians 5, Paul offered two similar contrasts—a contrast between darkness and light and a contrast between foolishness and wisdom. Here Paul goes on to contrast being drunk with wine versus being filled with the Spirit. Darkness and foolishness, he says, are marks of drunkenness. Being filled with the Spirit is a mark of wisdom and light.

God has called us to a life of spiritual intoxication.

The depressant versus the Stimulant

William Jennings Bryan, a teetotaler and a devout Christian politician who ran for president three times (1896, 1900, and 1908), once came up with a creative way to avoid drinking alcohol when asked to give a toast in honor of a victorious admiral. "The admiral has won a great victory on water," Bryan said, raising his water glass, "and I will therefore toast him with water. When the admiral wins a victory on champagne, I will toast him with champagne."

Different Christians hold differing views on alcohol. In fact, Christians have debated "to drink or not to drink" for two thousand years. Some believe that Jesus, who turned water into wine at the wedding in Cana, blessed the drinking of wine in moderation. Other Christians believe that biblical warnings against drunkenness are absolute, and that if a Christian drinks at all, he might cause a "weaker brother" to stumble. As Paul writes in Romans 14:21, "It is good not to eat meat or drink wine or do anything that causes your brother to stumble."

I'm not interested in adding my views to a debate that has already been raging for so many years. I am interested only in what the Word of God is saying to us here in Ephesians 5. What Paul talks about here is not drinking per se but drunkenness.

It's important to understand the cultural context in which Paul writes these words. In that pagan culture, drunkenness was closely associated with the worship of idols. This type of drunkenness produced an ecstatic emotional experience that the pagans believed was a sense of oneness with their gods. Like many people today, the first-century pagans sought religious fulfillment and spiritual highs through drunkenness and sexual immorality.

That is the context in which Paul writes Ephesians. He says, in effect, "Now that you are Christians, you don't need to come under the influence of alcohol to get your religious experience. Instead, place yourself under the influence and power of the Holy Spirit. Drunkenness in pagan worship causes you to lose control. But the fullness of the Holy Spirit will give you a sober, rational mind."

Many people think that alcohol is a stimulant, but it is actually a depressant. The high that many people feel while drunk is a result of the fact that alcohol depresses the judgment centers of the brain and reduces a person's social inhibitions. That's why people often do things while drunk that they deeply regret once they are sober.

By contrast, the fullness of the Holy Spirit is a stimulant to good judgment. Drunkenness dehumanizes people, but the fullness of the Holy Spirit makes you Christlike—the Spirit lifts you toward the ultimate role model of human perfection. Drunkenness numbs the judgment centers of your brain, but the fullness of the Holy Spirit gives you wisdom, discernment, good judgment, balanced thinking, and the power to act rationally and effectively in any situation.

How to be filled with the Spirit

What does it mean to be filled with the Holy Spirit? Before we answer that question, let's look at what the fullness of the Holy Spirit is *not.*

1. To be filled with the Holy Spirit does *not* mean that you get zapped and are instantly a first-class Christian.
2. To be filled with the Holy Spirit does *not* mean the same as being indwelt by the Holy Spirit. Romans 8:9 makes it clear that *every* Christian is indwelt by the Holy Spirit. But not every Christian is filled with the Holy Spirit.
3. To be filled with the Holy Spirit is *not* the same as being baptized by the Holy Spirit. Every believer has been baptized with the Holy Spirit at the moment of conversion. The fact that some believers quench the Holy Spirit and grieve the Holy Spirit does not stop the Holy Spirit from indwelling them.
4. To be filled with the Holy Spirit is *not* the same as being sealed with the Holy Spirit. Being sealed by the Holy Spirit is a declaration of God's ownership of the believer. This concept came from the time when people would seal the owner's name on merchandise to ensure its quality.
5. The filling of the Holy Spirit is *not* getting the Holy Spirit in installments. God does not parcel out the Holy Spirit. The Bible never commands the believer to be baptized by the Holy Spirit, sealed by the Holy Spirit, or indwelt by the Holy Spirit because that's something God does to the believer at the moment that person comes to Christ.

Ephesians 5:18 contains a specific command: "And do not get drunk with wine, for that is debauchery, but *be filled with the Spirit.*" This is not a suggestion or a recommendation. This is not one option among many. It is a command.

We cannot fulfill God's will for our lives without being filled with the Holy Spirit. We cannot obey the Word of God daily without being filled with the Holy Spirit. We cannot faithfully serve God without being continuously filled with the Holy Spirit. We cannot confidently resist temptation and have victory in our lives without being continuously filled with the Holy Spirit.

We cannot submit to one another. We cannot have peace with one another. We cannot in honor prefer one another. We cannot "in humility count others more significant than [ourselves]" (Philippians 2:3) without being filled, moment by moment, with the Holy Spirit.

So what does it mean to be filled with the Holy Spirit? It means to be totally under the control of the Spirit. It means that I get up every morning and pray, *Lord, you own me 100 percent. I place myself under the total control of your Holy Spirit.* And then I renew that prayer hourly or as often as needed throughout the day.

Is it possible to be filled with the Holy Spirit at all times, every day? I don't want to say it's impossible, but I do know that I fail and all other Christians I know say they fail too. In our fallenness, we stumble into sin again and again, no matter how much we sincerely want to please God. We say things and do things and think things we don't want to say or do or think. But we do not have to remain mired in our failure. We can renew our commitment to be filled with the Holy Spirit again and again. We can continually resubmit ourselves to the leading and control of God's Spirit.

Some people make a sincere decision to place God in the driver's seat of their lives at 7:00 a.m., but by 9:00 a.m., God is in the passenger seat and the self is in the driver's seat. Unless you surrender your life continuously to the Spirit's control, every moment of every day, you will live a defeated life. If you are experiencing spiritual defeat right now, you can turn your defeat into victory. Every time you are tempted to take back control of your life, return to God in prayer and submit yourself once more to the Spirit's control.

The grammatical construction of the original Greek text of Paul's letter is often very important to Paul's meaning. His command to be continuously filled with the Holy Spirit is stated in the passive voice of the imperative mood. This command is in the imperative mood because it is a must. This command is in the passive voice because all you need to do is be willing to submit to the Spirit's control. If it is something you have to exert, it would have been in the active voice.

Every married couple knows that the strength of their marriage is not in what happened in the past or what will happen in the future; it is in what happens right now, in the present. It's the same principle as the filling of the Holy Spirit. What truly matters is not what you did in the past or what you might do in the future; it's what you do right now that counts.

The filling of the Holy Spirit is not like filling a cup with water. The word *filling* here has the connotation of wind filling the sail of a ship and moving the ship forward. It's like salt penetrating deep into the food and giving it its full flavor. The filling of the Holy Spirit can be compared with being filled with sorrow or filled with anger. It doesn't mean that the person is like a cup filled with a liquid substance. It means the person is immersed, permeated, and moved along by what fills him.

To be filled with the Holy Spirit is to be totally dominated and controlled by the Holy Spirit. And to be filled and dominated by the Spirit is to be conscious of the presence of Jesus at every moment of every day. A person who is filled with the Spirit is conscious of the presence of Jesus when he or she is alone in the wilderness or surrounded by a crowd, when lost in quiet reflection or engaged in the fast-paced pressures of life. Being filled with the Spirit means that we include Jesus in every action we take and every decision we make.

The evidence of the filling of the Spirit

Finally, the apostle Paul describes the evidence of being filled by the Holy Spirit. What is that evidence?

> addressing one another in psalms and hymns and spiritual songs, singing and making melody to the Lord with your heart, giving thanks always and for everything to God the Father in the name of our Lord Jesus Christ (5:19-20).

Paul tells us that the person who is filled with the Spirit will always have a melody in his heart and a song on his lips. When we are constantly being filled with the Spirit, we will be filled with praise and thanksgiving to the Lord, even in tough times.

Paul writes that we should speak to one another with psalms, hymns, and spiritual songs. Some songs and psalms are designed for us to sing to one another—songs that say, "Let us worship the Lord," or "Bow down before him," or "Come into his presence." And there are other songs that we offer direct to Jesus—"Great are you, Lord," or "Blessed be your name," or "Thank you, Lord."

Some people focus too much on the technicalities of music, others on the artistry of music, and still others on the style of music. I can honestly tell you that I love them all. If the song is biblically sound, honoring to the Lord, and it invokes praise and thanks to him, then I will sing that song until I deafen everybody around me! Whether we can carry a tune in a bucket or not, God wants to hear sincere praise from our hearts and our lips.

When God puts something on my heart to pray for, and I know this prayer is consistent with the Word and the will of God, I don't even offer a petition—I just thank God, again and again, for what he is about to do. I don't have to see the outcome; I thank God in advance.

I think this is how Jesus responded to God the Father when he stood before the tomb of Lazarus. His friend still lay dead in the tomb, yet Jesus said, "Father, I thank you that you have heard me" (John 11:41). He knew what the Father was about to do, and he was grateful to the Father even before a single cell of Lazarus's body had moved from death to life.

A medieval legend tells us that God sent two angels to Earth to gather the prayers of his people. One angel was sent to gather petitions. The other was sent to gather prayers of thanksgiving. The angel responsible for gathering petitions was not able to carry them all back to heaven in one load. But the angel who carried thanksgiving prayers carried them all back in one hand.

What are your prayers like? Are your prayers laden with petitions but light on gratitude? Do you pray only when there is a desperate need in your life? Or do you exert the same energy in giving thanks to the Lord as when you offer petitions and pleas for help? If you are a parent, you know how a thankful child brings joy to your heart. How much more does a thankful believer bring joy to the heart of God?

When your life is characterized by psalms, hymns, and spiritual songs and prayers of thanksgiving, you show that you are being continually controlled by the Holy Spirit. That is what it means to not be drunk with wine, but filled with the Spirit.

10

God's Plan for Marriage

Ephesians 5:21-33

A young lady went to the post office to select special commemorative stamps for her wedding invitations. She examined one stamp design after another, and couldn't find any stamps that depicted a theme appropriate for her wedding invitations. Finally, she looked at one sheet of commemoratives and said, "That's it!"

It was a John Paul Jones commemorative stamp bearing the admiral's famous rallying cry, "I have not yet begun to fight!"

For all too many people, marriage is a scene of battle. But marriage, as God created it and intended it to be, is a picture of Christ and his church. God planned for the love of a husband and wife to symbolize the love between Christ and his church. Because that is one of God's key purposes for marriage, Satan has worked hard at destroying marriage and eradicating the symbolism of Christian marriage from our minds.

There is no greater deception that Satan has perpetrated on our society than the deception he has foisted upon us about marriage and family. Look around at the prevalence in our culture and our media of casual sex, homosexuality, and infidelity. Typical of this media assault is a TV show on the ABC network (owned by the Walt Disney Company!) called *GCB*. Those letters stand for *Good Christian*... and a word I refuse to put in print. This show depicts church-going Christians in Dallas engaging in adultery, homosexuality, self-righteous judgment, addiction to pornography, addiction to plastic surgery, and more. This is clearly a satanic assault on the image of the Christian church, designed by our enemy to portray Christian marriage as nothing more than a hotbed of hypocrisy and infidelity.

This is not to say that such behavior can't be found in Christian marriages and Christian churches. To our sorrow and shame, we must admit that there is sin in our midst. But it is a satanic slander to depict Christian marriage as *essentially and primarily* a pious and hypocritical sham hiding a *Desperate Housewives* reality. Genuine, Christ-centered, God-honoring Christian marriages do exist, and they are the norm in the church. Hollywood is determined to tear down godly marriages and replace them with militant feminism, rampant immorality, and serial divorce.

The lie of "oppressive" Christian marriage

One of the great satanic deceptions about marriage is that God's blueprint for marriage and the family is somehow oppressive toward women. For example, radical feminist Susan Brownmiller claims that marriage originated in rape and that primitive women chose one rapist as a husband to gain protection from other rapists.[9] The wonderful foundation that God our Maker has ordained for the joy and fulfillment of the family has been denigrated as nothing more than an outgrowth of primitive caveman cruelty. The same serpent who once asked Eve, "Did God really mean that?" now deceives millions, misleading them into believing that God's plan for a husband to lovingly exercise spiritual headship, and for the wife to faithfully affirm him in that headship, is oppressive and ought to be rejected.

We can look around us and see what occurs when we reject God's plan for marriage: divorce, emotionally scarred children, and social collapse. According to the National Fatherhood Initiative, U.S. prisons are filled with overwhelmingly male populations who grew up in fatherless homes. Of all men in prisons, 70 percent of long-term inmates, 72 percent of adolescent murderers, and 60 percent of convicted rapists came from fatherless homes.[10] We can draw at least two startling conclusions from these facts:

First, while militant feminists slander marriage as an outgrowth of rape, the facts show that rapists overwhelmingly come from fatherless homes, not two-parent families. The covenant of marriage is actually a powerful *preventative* to the crime of rape.

Second, criminal populations overwhelmingly come from fatherless homes—what we used to call "broken homes." If every family unit in America were established and built on the biblical foundation of marriage, it is reasonable to suppose that we would dramatically slash crime rates in America—perhaps not by 70 percent (there are undoubtedly other factors that lead people into a life of crime), but certainly by a significant amount.

Many militant feminists have misinterpreted and twisted the teachings of the Bible, and all too many Christians have allowed themselves to be intimidated and embarrassed by the very passages of Scripture that reveal God's secret for happiness in a marriage relationship. These militants bring misery on themselves and spread that misery to others.

Let's not be intimidated or silenced by the deceptions of Satan or the corrosive systems of this world. Let's take a stand for biblical truth and declare that we will not be ashamed of the gospel of Jesus Christ.

Liberating, not oppressive

What is the greatest force for women's equality and liberation in the history of humanity? Without question it is Jesus himself and the Christian gospel. In the four Gospels, we see that Jesus treated women with respect and elevated their status (see Matthew 9, 26; Mark 14; Luke 7; John 4, 8). The New Testament boldly declares that both men and women are equal in the sight of God: "There is neither Jew nor Greek, there is neither slave nor free, there is no male and female, for you are all one in Christ Jesus" (Galatians 3:28). The New Testament also declares that God loves men and women equally, and that both husband and wife are to submit to one another, as we read in Ephesians 5:

> submitting to one another out of reverence for Christ.
>
> Wives, submit to your own husbands, as to the Lord. For the husband is the head of the wife even as Christ is the head of the church, his body, and is himself its Savior. Now as the church submits to Christ, so also wives should submit in everything to their husbands (5:21-24).

The enemies of the Bible ignore verse 21, which is foundational to the rest of the passage. Before Paul can go on to talk about the different roles husbands and wives are called to by God, he writes verse 21, in which he equalizes both men and women before God.

Let's put Paul's teaching into its cultural context. When Paul wrote this letter, there were three cultures that mingled and sometimes collided in that region. There was the ancient Jewish culture, the Roman culture, and the Greek culture. All three cultures relegated women to second-class, subservient status.

In the Jewish culture at that time, women were treated as *things*, not full-fledged people with human rights. That's why a Jewish man prayed daily, "I thank you, Lord, that I am a Jew, not a Gentile; free, not a slave; and that I am a man and not a woman."

Women fared no better in the Greek culture. They were kept out of sight in total obedience to the husband. Xenophon, a Greek writer, said that the reason women were kept out of view was so that they "might see as little as possible, hear as little as possible, and ask as little as possible."[11]

The Roman culture didn't treat women any better. Women had no rights whatsoever, and the law considered a woman to be the equivalent of a child. The Roman philosopher Seneca observed that women "were married to be divorced and divorced to be married."[12]

Into this cultural maelstrom, the apostle Paul comes with a radical new message and astonishing good news for women: men and women are to submit to one another out of reverence for Christ. That was revolutionary thinking—and true women's liberation! That is freedom and genuine equality in the eyes of God. The fact that the Bible assigns different roles for husbands and wives is liberating, not oppressing.

A good analogy for the differences between the husband's role and the wife's role would be the three branches of the U.S. government. According to the U.S. Constitution, our three branches of government—executive (the president), legislative (the Congress), and judicial (the Supreme Court)—have coequal powers. They don't have the *same* powers, and they don't perform the same *functions*; each has a unique role. The Congress must submit to the president in order for a bill to be signed into law. The Congress and the president must submit to the will of the court if the court finds a law unconstitutional. Yet the court cannot make laws like the Congress or negotiate treaties like the president. Each branch has its assigned role, each mutually submits to the other two branches, and no one branch is superior or inferior to the other two.

The same is true in marriage. A husband and wife each have unique roles. They mutually submit to each other. Neither the husband nor the wife is superior or inferior to the other. They are coequal.

Why are we drowning in a tidal wave of marriage books, seminars, and counselors today? Isn't it because we simply don't like God's blueprint for a joyous marriage, and we have rejected it? Isn't it because we think that if we would just read the latest book on marriage, we would gain some new insight or principle that would be the key to a happy marriage?

But we don't need a new insight or principle. We simply need to obey the insights and principles God has already given us in his Word, and especially here in Ephesians 5.

Mutual submission—not a power struggle

In the preceding verses, Paul wrote about the filling of the Holy Spirit. There is a logical connection between Paul's teaching about being filled with the Holy Spirit and his teaching about God's plan for Christian marriage. Only those who are constantly being filled with the Holy Spirit can live out God's blueprint for marriage.

We must continually submit to the Spirit's leading in order to mutually submit to each other in marriage. Without the filling of the Spirit, we will simply be incapable, in our fallen human flesh, of accepting the roles God has assigned to us in marriage. There will be no mutual forgiveness, no mutual submission, and no mutual sacrifice.

"Wives, submit to your own husbands, as to the Lord," Paul writes. People who do not have the filling of the Spirit read those words and completely misunderstand. They think that Paul is telling wives to knuckle under and become doormats for their husbands. Nothing could be further from the truth.

Christian marriage is a partnership, and the husband and the wife bring different contributions, different roles to the relationship. The wife brings a distinct role in which she will receive her fulfillment, and it's a role the husband cannot fulfill. You cannot separate the wife's submission from the husband's headship. The two are inextricably linked.

Remember that Christian marriage is a picture of the relationship between Christ and the church. If you remember this truth, then Christian marriage makes sense; if you forget this truth, you will never understand Christian marriage. Headship in the Christian home is inseparable from the model of Christ. The submission of the wife to the headship of the husband echoes the submission of the church to Christ.

How did Jesus Christ exercise his headship? By serving, giving, sacrificing, and putting the church, his bride, ahead of his own interests. He exercised his headship by dying for the church. Who wouldn't want to submit to this kind of loving headship? What wife wouldn't want to submit to a husband who was totally Christlike in everything he did and said? That is why Paul goes on to write:

> Husbands, love your wives, as Christ loved the church and gave himself up for her, that he might sanctify her, having cleansed her by the washing of water with the word, so that he might present the church to himself in splendor, without spot or wrinkle or any such thing, that she might be holy and without blemish. In the same way husbands should love their wives as their own bodies. He who loves his wife loves himself. For no one ever hated his own flesh, but nourishes and cherishes it, just as Christ does the church, because we are members of his body. "Therefore a man shall leave his father and mother and hold fast to his wife, and the two shall become one flesh." This mystery is profound, and I am saying that it refers to Christ and the church. However, let each one of you love his wife as himself, and let the wife see that she respects her husband (5:25-33).

Christian marriage is not a power struggle—it's mutual love and mutual submission. Some marriages end up being a power struggle because either the wife refuses to submit as unto the Lord, or the husband refuses to lead and love like Jesus—or both!

God's plan for marriage is not for the exaltation of the husband and the oppression of the wife. God's plan for marriage elevates and ennobles the roles of both men and women, as it symbolically depicts the unique love relationship between Christ and his bride, the church.

The power of love

I think it's significant that Paul uses twice as many words to address husbands as he does to address wives. I believe Paul needs to go into greater depth and detail in addressing men because submitting by loving is a more demanding challenge than submitting by following. You can submit without loving, but it's impossible to love without submitting.

Whenever you love someone, you place your beloved's needs and welfare above your own. You place your beloved's desires and comforts ahead of your own. Notice that Paul not only says that a husband is to love his wife as Christ loved the church, but he repeats this principle three times.

What did Christ do for his bride, the church? He left his glory, he came to a world that hated him and cursed him, and he allowed that world to crucify him. Jesus set aside his own needs, wants, and desires so that he could redeem and save his bride, the church. Love wants only the best for the beloved. Love cannot stand idly by, watching the beloved suffer harm. Love can never be passive when the beloved is in danger.

It should be obvious that love never entices or coerces the beloved to do anything wrong or sinful. When Paul writes, "wives should submit in everything to their husbands," it is understood, it is obvious, that Paul is saying that wives should submit in every *good* thing. Just as Christ would never command the church to sin, a loving husband would never demand that his wife should sin. If a husband ever asks his wife to lie, steal, cheat, or sin in any other way, she has every right to refuse him. Every Christian has a duty to *obey*

God rather than men, if the commands of God and men are ever in conflict.

Paul describes a husband's love for his wife as being like the love of Christ for us. "Christ loved the church and gave himself up for her," Paul writes, "that he might sanctify her, having cleansed her by the washing of water with the word, so that he might present the church to himself in splendor, without spot or wrinkle or any such thing, that she might be holy and without blemish." Through this sanctification process, the Lord does for the church what no amount of adornment, jewelry, nail polish, makeup, or even Botox could do: Jesus removes all wrinkles, spots, and blemishes from the church through the inner filling of the Holy Spirit. God's Spirit continuously cleanses us and sanctifies us until we—in a state of absolute and stunning purity—see Jesus face-to-face.

What wife in her right mind would not want to submit to such an awe-inspiring love? What wife would not delight to honor, respect, and follow that kind of all-embracing love?

God's blueprint for a joyous marriage

Let me summarize Paul's teaching by giving you a five-point outline of God's blueprint for a joyous marriage:

1. Christian marriage is based on mutual submission. Paul writes that the foundation of a joyous marriage is "submitting to one another out of reverence for Christ." *Submission* is a beautiful word, not a dirty word. The essence of the Lord's work on earth was submission. Though he is equal with God, Jesus did not consider equality with God something to cling to. He surrendered his prerogatives as God, and he submitted to his Father and obeyed him. Did his submission to the Father make him inferior to the Father? Of course not. Submission does not take away our worth or our equality. But submission does enable beautiful things to happen in our lives.

2. A wife's submission is submission to a lover, not oppression by a boss. The world does not understand this kind of submission. That's why it is critically important that you and I study God's Word and seek to understand these issues from a heavenly perspective, not a worldly perspective. Once we have a biblical understanding of submission, we are able to understand and fulfill our roles as Christians in submission to Christ and as mutually submitted husbands and wives.

3. A husband's headship is a matter of serving, not lording. In his description of the husband's headship, Paul repeatedly uses the word *love*. "Husbands, love your wives, as Christ loved the church...Husbands should love their wives as their own bodies. He who loves his wife loves himself...Let each one of you love his wife as himself." Love your wife as Christ loved the church, nourish her as Christ nourishes the church, and lead her as Christ leads his church. Be a servant, not a tyrant.

4. A husband's love is demonstrated in action. There are a number of verbs—action words—that describe how a husband should demonstrate love for his wife. Paul says that a husband must love his wife, give himself for her, sanctify his wife, cleanse her and wash her, make her holy, present her, nourish her, and cherish her. Love is not a feeling. Love is action.

5. A wife's submission is nothing but a natural, rational response to a husband's extravagant, selfless, self-sacrificing love. Far from being a response of fear toward an oppressor (which is the worldly view of submission), a wife's submission is the response you would expect from a woman whose husband loves her as Christ loved the church. If you are a wife, God is calling you to respond to your husband's love by lifting him up, encouraging him, and respecting him—not beating him down. If you are a husband, God is calling you to put your wife's needs ahead of your own and to love your wife as Christ loved the church.

The essence of a Christian marriage is Christ's relationship to us as believers. We, the church, are his bride. Until every husband and every wife learn to give themselves totally to Christ and experience the joy that comes from submission to the Lord Jesus, they will never know the joy of giving themselves totally to each other in Christian marriage.

If you want to find yourself in a joyful Christian marriage, then lose yourself in Christ. Lose yourself in a mutually submissive marriage relationship.

Submission is the essence of the Christian faith. It's the secret of fulfillment. It's the ultimate in true contentment in life. Joy in marriage, and in the Christian life, comes as we give ourselves fully to each other and fully to Christ, trusting without fear, serving without reservation, and loving with the selfless love of Christ himself.

11

God's Plan for Raising Children

Ephesians 6:1-4

In the ancient Roman culture, a father had absolute power over his wife and children. He could sell them as slaves. He could force them to work in the field in chains. He could inflict pain and even death on them with the full approval of the Roman government.

The power of a father over his children extended throughout their lifetime. Even when a son became a grown man, even if he became a government official, even if the state crowned his achievements with honors, he remained under his father's absolute power until his father died.

The Roman culture practiced a form of "late-term abortion" that took place immediately after the baby was born alive. The newborn infant was placed at his father's feet. If the father stooped and lifted the child, it meant that he wished to keep the baby. But if the father turned and walked away, the baby was condemned to death.

During the apostle Paul's time, unwanted children were often left in the Roman Forum. The abandoned children became the property of anyone who cared to pick them up and take them home. Some would take these children home and raise them as their own. But far more often, those who took the children (often by night) did so out of a profit motive: these children would eventually be sold or put to work as slaves in the fields or the brothels.

In Ephesians 5, we saw how Jesus and the Christian faith truly liberated women and elevated their status. Here in Ephesians 6, we see that the same is true for children. Jesus and Christianity brought a degree of love, respect, and nurturing for children that had been unknown in the ancient world up to that time. Even in ancient Jewish culture, children were often mistreated and scorned—until the Lord Jesus came and said, "Let the little children come to me and do not hinder them, for to such belongs the kingdom of heaven" (Matthew 19:14).

This was a radical statement, a revolutionary concept, in those days. For Paul to acknowledge children and give them their own section in his letter to the Ephesians is a clear indication of how much the church's influence and the Christian faith began to impact Roman society.

A commandment with a promise

In Ephesians 6, Paul begins by teaching children that, since Jesus Christ has lifted them up and loved them, blessing them with dignity, they must not use their improved status as an excuse for rudeness or disobedience to parents. He writes:

> Children, obey your parents in the Lord, for this is right. "Honor your father and mother" (this is the first commandment with a promise), "that it may go well with you and that you may live long in the land" (6:1-3).

Paul does not engage in coddling or spoiling the child. He bluntly states, "Children, obey your parents in the Lord, for this is right." He doesn't say, "Obey your parents if you feel like it. Obey your parents if you agree with them. Obey your parents if their demands seem reasonable to you." He says, "Obey them, for this is right."

This is a command to Christian children in a Christian home who are living under their parents' roof. When children become adults and leave their parents and cleave to their spouses, they must still honor their parents, though they are not necessarily required to obey them. They are to use their parents as a point of reference, but not to be in total submission to them. They are to care for their parents, but out of respect and honor, not a misplaced sense of guilt.

Why is it important for children living under their parents' roof to obey their parents? When children are taught early on to obey their parents, they will also learn obedience to the Lord. Children who learn to submit to parental authority will much more readily submit to God's authority. When children are trained to respond positively to their parents' direction, they will become adults who respond positively to their heavenly Father's direction.

I have many joyful opportunities to meet with young parents in our church, and I often remind them that our children do not really belong to us. They belong to the Lord. He entrusts our children to us to nurture and train them on his behalf. But our children are actually *his* children.

Parents are stewards, not owners. We do not own money or possessions; God has placed these things in our hands for safekeeping, and we are to manage these things on the Lord's behalf. So it is with our children. The authority we have as parents is actually proxy authority from God. That is why children are to obey their parents in the Lord.

What does it mean to obey and honor your parents? It means to highly value them, esteem them, and respect them. The obedience or honor that children owe to parents is so important to God that he placed this command among the Ten Commandments—and he accompanied that commandment with a promise.

The promise is that when we honor, respect, revere, and obey our parents, God has a special blessing in store for us. In the Old Testament, that promise was tied to living long in the Land of Promise. But in the New Testament, the blessings are without limit. God knew that the child who would honor, respect, and obey his or her parents would grow up to honor, respect, and obey God. Obedience to God causes true blessings to multiply.

You may struggle with these principles because you have struggled with your parents. Perhaps you are an adult now, and you have always—even in adulthood—been at odds with your parents. In the process of trying to break free from parents who may have been dysfunctional or even hurtful to you, perhaps you have been disrespectful and dishonoring toward them. If so, I encourage you to go to them and say, "God commands that I honor and respect you. As an adult, I don't have to obey you—but I don't want to treat you with disrespect. I want to obey God and obey his Word. So I ask you to forgive me for my past disrespect, and from now on, I want to have a better relationship with you."

Your parents may respond favorably to your words—or, if they are really dysfunctional, they may heap even *more* abuse on you. That doesn't matter. Make up your mind that you will show respect even if you are not respected. You will show honor even if you are not honored in return. You will make peace, as much as the responsibility rests with you. If you honor your parents, even if your efforts go unrequited, God will honor you for your faithfulness and obedience. He will pour out incredible blessings on your life.

A commandment to parents

It was a revolutionary statement Paul made when he elevated the status of children in this passage. And his next statement was even more revolutionary and shocking in that ancient first-century culture:

> Fathers, do not provoke your children to anger, but bring them up in the discipline and instruction of the Lord (6:4).

The Greek word rendered *fathers* in this verse was used, on occasion, for *parents* (see Hebrews 11:23). Paul is saying, in effect, "Parents, don't exasperate your children. Instead, train them and discipline them in the instruction of the Lord."

Many people today use personal trainers to coach them in their diet, physical exercise, or physiotherapy regimens. Good trainers do not come cheap, but their advice and motivational support are extremely valuable. They show us the right way to eat and exercise, and help us avoid the wrong way of training. Good trainers help us make the daily effort that produces incremental changes in our bodies that, over time, lead to energy, strength, and good health.

As parents, we are the personal trainers of our children. Parents make a difference by the way they train and motivate their children day after day. By instructing, disciplining, and motivating their children, parents help kids make those incremental changes in their character and faith that lead to a balanced intellect, healthy emotions, strong values and character traits, and an attractive personality.

Christian parents understand that this life is a spiritual battlefield and that they need to prepare their children for spiritual warfare. It's important to teach children how to handle money, how to avoid peer pressure and drugs, how to succeed in school and in their careers, but if you do not train your children in spiritual warfare, in strategies for relying on God's Word, God's Spirit, and prayer, then you leave your children wide open to Satan's attack. Your spiritual preparation and training of your children may spell the difference between winning and losing the spiritual battles of this life.

Paul wants us to know that one of the key principles in preparing our children for spiritual battle is to avoid exasperating and provoking our children. I want to share with you some of the lessons I've learned from my own failures as a Christian father, or from the ways my own parents (with the best of intentions) sometimes exasperated me.

If there's one thing I know about parenting, it's that the vast majority of parents truly love their children and raise their children with the best of intentions. Yes, there are evil parents, neglectful or abusive parents, and parents with disordered and sociopathic personalities who do great harm in many young lives. But these are the minority. Most parents love their children and want the best for them. But because parents are human, we all inevitably fail and occasionally provoke and exasperate our children. Here, then, are some insights I've learned in how not to provoke our children, but to raise them as Christ himself would raise them:

1. Give your children gradually increasing responsibilities. To do this well, you must know the appropriate stage in your child's development for each level of responsibility. If you put the same restrictions on a child when he is thirteen as you did when he was six, you will exasperate him. So allow your children to make their own decisions in a gradual way, giving them more and more freedom an inch at a time. Above all, give them the freedom to fail. Overprotecting your children will not only provoke them, but will rob them of their ability to make their own decisions and become self-sufficient adults. Children need to make their own mistakes. They learn the most lasting lessons by incurring the consequences of their mistakes and poor decisions.

2. Avoid favoritism. This does not mean you should treat all your children alike—a five-year-old and a thirteen-year-old should not have exactly the same privileges and responsibilities. But even though you can't treat your children exactly alike, you can treat them all without favoritism.

In the story of Isaac and Rebecca, we see how Isaac favored Esau while Rebecca favored Jacob. The favoritism of the parents for the sons produced heartbreaking, murderous hatred between Esau and Jacob. Later, Jacob followed the example of his parents and showed flagrant favoritism toward his son Joseph—and once again, the result was heartbreak for Jacob and murderous hatred among his sons. Favoritism stirs up resentment and bitterness in a child's heart. Favoritism is one of the sins a parent may commit that truly provokes and exasperates a child.

3. Don't push your children into areas where they lack aptitude or ability. It's healthy to expose your children to many activities and experiences, from sports to music to science to ministry. As you expose your kids to these experiences, study them and notice how they respond. Do they enjoy the activity? Do they excel at it? If the answer is no, don't push them, don't frustrate them, and above all, don't try to live out your athletic or musical dreams through your children. Just because you loved dance or painting or baseball as a child doesn't mean that your children should follow in your footsteps. Pushing children into an activity they hate or cannot perform will only provoke and exasperate them. Find out which direction your children are naturally inclined, then encourage them and cheer them on in that direction.

4. Don't remind your children of their limitations or failures. Instead, focus on the things they excel in. Affirm their talents and strengths. Above all, affirm their good character traits. Remind them that God gives everyone different gifts, and he does not want us to compare ourselves with others. Every child needs encouragement and approval from parents. If we give them that approval in the areas where they excel, we will avoid exasperating and provoking them—and we will motivate them to succeed.

Child psychologists Michael Thompson and Dan Kindlon tell a story about a father who taught his six-year-old son how to ski.

While father and son were on the slopes together, the boy repeatedly fell and picked himself up, struggling valiantly to learn the art of skiing. No matter how many times the boy fell, his dad cheered him on. Finally, in the late afternoon, it was time to return to the lodge for some hot cocoa. The dad asked his son, "What did you enjoy most about skiing?" The boy's eyes lit up and he said, "Watching you watch me ski!"

"What really mattered to the boy," the authors concluded, "was not how well or poorly he skied but what his dad thought of him."[13] That principle holds true in the life of every child. So to avoid exasperating and provoking your children, continually cheer them on and avoid criticizing them or reminding them of their limitations and failures.

5. Never suggest that your children are a burden or a nuisance. A well-known evangelical leader once told me that before he became a Christian, he felt his children just got in the way of his worldly ambitions to achieve great things in his life—and he told his children that! These words created deep wounds of resentment and exasperation in his children. After this man gave his life to Christ, he realized how much he had hurt his children, and he spent the rest of his life trying to undo the damage his thoughtless words had caused.

Always remind your children that they are a gift from God. Our Father and Creator knew our children before they were born—and even before the foundation of the world. Tell your children how honored you are that God entrusted them to you and allowed you to "bring them up in the discipline and instruction of the Lord" (6:4).

6. Don't remind your children of how good they have it now compared with how life was in your day. You can thank God for providing things for your children that you didn't have growing up, but avoid condemning or criticizing your children by saying, "You've got it so easy," or "You don't know how lucky you are." Our kids enjoy many conveniences we didn't have, but they also face pressures and dangers that we didn't face. Each generation has its own burdens to deal with.

It's okay to joke with our kids about the old days, of course. When my children were young, I'd tell them the standard tall tales about walking to school, trudging barefoot through the snow for miles and miles. And of course, my children were never fooled. "Dad," they'd say with a sly grin, "we didn't know that it snowed in Egypt!"

7. Don't punish children by withholding love. Children don't understand the silent treatment. If you give a child the "deep freeze" treatment, that child will feel unwanted and unloved—and exasperated.

I once heard of a preacher who recalled that when he was a boy and did something wrong, his mother turned her back on him and refused to talk to him or acknowledge him. He went on to make this application from his childhood story: "This is how God deals with us every time we sin. He turns his back on us and refuses to have anything to do with us."

This is horrible theology! How tragic that this preacher transferred his mother's behavior to God and assumed that withholding love is normal and natural for parents and for God. His boyhood exasperation twisted his theology, his image of God, and his preaching from the pulpit.

"Fathers and mothers," Paul pleads with us, "do not provoke your children to anger, but bring them up in the discipline and instruction of the Lord."

The key is balance

I have learned that one of the most important words in parenting is *balance*. When you over-praise and over-empower your kids, they tend to develop a sense of entitlement. They become spoiled. When you under-affirm and under-empower them, they tend to become insecure and lacking in confidence.

The answer to these two extremes, of course, is balance.

Someone once said, "The true meaning of life is to plant trees under whose shade you do not expect to sit." As parents, we plant trees of character traits, good habits, wisdom, and spiritual strength to give our children cooling shade in the days and years to come. If you plant a tree that is lush and rich, watered by the Word of God, your children will sit under it and delight themselves in its shade and enjoy its fruit for a lifetime.

And even after you are gone, they will remember you and thank you and bless you for raising them in the discipline and instruction of the Lord.

12

God's Plan for Your Workplace

Ephesians 6:5-9

William Wilberforce was born to power and privilege in England. Educated at Cambridge, he was eager to make a name for himself as a politician—not in order to improve living conditions for his fellow citizens but to feed his own ego and be invited to all the best dinner parties. Elected to Parliament in 1780, he later admitted that his early years in Parliament were wasted: "I did nothing—nothing to any purpose."

In late 1785, he went through a period of deep soul-searching and depression. He questioned the meaning of his life. "I am sure that no human creature could suffer more than I did for some months," he wrote. On Easter morning 1786, at age twenty-six, Wilberforce committed his life to Jesus Christ and experienced a life-changing spiritual rebirth.

As a Christian, he began taking life and politics seriously. He stopped drinking alcohol, stopped going to dinner parties, and began focusing on two causes that God had called him to—evangelizing the lost for Jesus Christ and abolishing the slave trade. Years later, he recalled, "So enormous, so dreadful, so irremediable did the [slave] trade's wickedness appear that my own mind was completely made up for abolition."

During that time, English slave traders were shipping between thirty-five thousand and fifty thousand Africans *every year* across the Atlantic. The practice of slavery became so essential to the economy of Europe and America that few people thought slavery could ever be abolished. But Wilberforce was committed to ending slavery in his lifetime.

Wilberforce spent time learning firsthand about the horrors of the slave trade from John Newton, a former ship's captain who left the slave trade in 1754 after converting to Christ. Newton had gone into the ministry and had written the hymn "Amazing Grace" in 1773. Newton, who was thirty-five years older than Wilberforce, became a mentor to the young politician, urging Wilberforce to use his influence in Parliament to make a difference for God and for human dignity.

So William Wilberforce fought hard in the Parliament, introducing a series of resolutions against slavery. But each resolution he introduced was blocked by powerful political blocs controlled by the slave merchants.

When Wilberforce refused to give up his crusade against slavery, his opponents launched a smear campaign against him, and his friends feared for his physical safety. He was also plagued by recurring illnesses that often kept him bedridden for weeks. His doctor prescribed a new drug to help him tolerate the pain—a drug called opium. The drug was so new that its addictive and mind-altering properties were not well known, and Wilberforce found himself addicted to this terrible narcotic.

In spite of all the obstacles and opposition he faced, Wilberforce finally achieved victory in 1807—twenty years after he began his antislavery campaign—when Parliament finally voted to abolish the slave trade throughout the British Empire. Wilberforce spent the rest of his years working to make sure that the antislavery laws were obeyed. He won a great victory just days before his death in July 1833 when he saw that an emancipation bill, freeing all remaining slaves in the British Empire, was approved in committee and guaranteed to win passage by Parliament.[14]

William Wilberforce was just one person, but he surrendered his will to the Spirit of God, and God used him to change the world. What is God waiting to do through your life right now?

The problem of slavery

At the same time that William Wilberforce was led by the Spirit to oppose the practice of slavery, other men were using God's Word to rationalize the slave trade. They claimed that God actually *endorsed* human slavery! A typical example of this view of Scripture and slavery was expressed by Jefferson Davis, the president of the Confederate States of America during the U.S. Civil War. He wrote that slavery "was established by decree of Almighty God...It is sanctioned in the Bible, in both Testaments, from Genesis to Revelation."[15]

In the next section of Ephesians 6, we come to one of the Scripture passages that many slave owners and slave traders of that time relied on to justify their cruel commerce in human flesh. It is important that we understand exactly what Paul was saying in this passage and why he said it:

> Bondservants, obey your earthly masters with fear and trembling, with a sincere heart, as you would Christ, not by the way of eye-service, as people-pleasers, but as bondservants of Christ, doing the will of God from the heart, rendering service with a good will as to the Lord and not

> to man, knowing that whatever good anyone does, this he will receive back from the Lord, whether he is a bondservant or is free. Masters, do the same to them, and stop your threatening, knowing that he who is both their Master and yours is in heaven, and that there is no partiality with him (6:5-9).

Critics of the Bible and opponents of the Christian faith often condemn the apostle Paul for writing these words. They claim that Paul should have told slaves *not* to obey their masters, but instead to rise up and revolt against their masters. These critics misunderstand the power of the gospel, the intent of the gospel, and the times in which Paul's letters were written.

When Paul wrote his letters under the inspiration of the Holy Spirit, there were an estimated sixty million slaves in the Roman Empire. The Romans had reached such a level of wealth, decadence, and arrogance that it was considered beneath the dignity of a Roman to do his own work. So the idle rich Romans used slaves—not merely as farm laborers, but as doctors, teachers, accountants, and secretaries.

While slavery in America was primarily a matter of race, slaves in the Roman Empire came from a variety of races, including people who were ethnically Roman. Many slaves were formerly free people who sold themselves into slavery to settle debts, children sold into slavery by impoverished parents, orphaned or abandoned children, or enslaved prisoners captured in war. Nowhere in the New Testament is slavery condemned as a social injustice or condoned as a social necessity. Slavery was so pervasive in the ancient world that it was simply accepted as a fact that could not be changed or even challenged.

Critics of the Bible who say that Paul should have openly attacked slavery and called for its abolition would have a different view if they lived with the boot of Rome on their necks. Anyone calling for an uprising against the Roman political and social regime risked a horrible death, including possible crucifixion. It's one thing to demand radical social change in a free society under the protection of the First Amendment. It's quite another thing to dare to speak out against the brutal Roman dictatorship.

The message of the Christian gospel has truly transformed societies, introducing to the global conversation concepts of justice, freedom, peacemaking, and compassion for the poor and oppressed. But nowhere in the New Testament do we see Christians being called to confront the governmental policies of the Roman Empire. The gospel transforms society by first transforming individuals, much as John Newton and William Wilberforce were transformed by the gospel. God then works through transformed individuals to change society.

Paul wrote his letters at a time when slavery was an unquestioned social norm. But as you read his letters, you find certain themes occurring again and again—themes of liberty, of love and charity, of brotherhood and equality. Paul wrote, for example, "There is neither Jew nor Greek, there is neither slave nor free, there is no male and female, for you are all one in Christ Jesus" (Galatians 3:28). And Jesus was the One who announced his mission on earth with these words from the prophet Isaiah:

> "The Spirit of the Lord is upon me,
> because he has anointed me
> to proclaim good news to the poor.
> He has sent me to proclaim liberty to the captives
> and recovering of sight to the blind,
> to set at liberty those who are oppressed,
> to proclaim the year of the Lord's favor."
> (Luke 4:18-19)

Concepts of liberty and equality are central to the Christian gospel—not as political slogans but as eternal spiritual realities. That is why the Christian faith had such a strong appeal among slaves in the Roman Empire. Many slaves converted to this new religion of Christianity because of its message of justice and freedom.

But Christianity was an outlawed religion in the Roman Empire. So Paul counseled his fellow believers, if they were slaves, to be peaceable and obedient so that further oppression would not be brought down on slaves and on other Christians. When Paul preached obedience to slave-masters, he didn't condone slavery. He was giving practical advice to prevent further suffering throughout the persecuted Christian community, among both enslaved and free Christians.

Throughout the New Testament, Paul teaches that when the heart is changed, when a life is committed to Christ, the social order cannot remain the same. The relationship between slaves and masters will eventually begin to mirror the relationship between believers and Christ.

And who would not want Christ for a master? He not only loves his servants perfectly and treats them as friends, but he adopts them and calls them his sons and daughters. He provides for their every need. He protects them from the wicked mastery of sin and Satan. He guards them and shelters them from the enemy of their souls. He names them in his will as coheirs with him.

The heart of the problem

The New Testament does not focus on outward reformation or restructuring political or social systems. The New Testament does not teach a gradual improvement of the human condition. The New Testament does not call for tinkering with the outward surface of life's issues.

The New Testament tells us that the real problem with the human condition is *a problem of the heart*. The heart needs radical surgery, not cosmetic surgery. The only way to truly transform society is by transforming human hearts. When the gospel of Jesus Christ penetrates human hearts, the people themselves change, their society changes, and their social and political systems begin to change as well.

Many Christians think that the only way to change society is through the political process. They want to radically alter society by imposing a social gospel on all of society by pulling the levers of worldly power. But you cannot change society into what it ought to be without calling individuals to transformation through Christ. If the human heart remains unchanged, wicked men will always find a way to oppress others.

Thanks to William Wilberforce and other Christian abolitionists of the nineteenth century, slavery has long been illegal in Western society. It is largely the enlightening power of the Christian gospel that has permeated our society, making it unthinkable and unacceptable that one person should own another person as property.

Slavery is, unfortunately, still commonplace in parts of the world that resist the Christian gospel. A special UN session on human slavery concludes that there are at least twenty-seven million slaves in the world today, including millions of girls who work as domestic servants and sex slaves. Forced workers carry out much of the construction work in Pakistan, Sudan, and Mauritania. In some parts of the world, children are forced to work in mines and factories, where they are subjected to dangerous working conditions and chemicals. Orphaned or abandoned boys work as jockeys in dangerous camel races in the United Arab Emirates. In parts of Asia, children are forced into prostitution at an early age, and in parts of Africa, children are trained as soldiers or are used as human landmine detectors.[16]

Here in the West, we have largely eradicated the scourge of human slavery by changing hearts and minds. Because of the Christian gospel, we view slavery as the most abhorrent practice imaginable—an outrage that we would not accept in our society.

How then should we apply Paul's teachings in Ephesians 6:5-9 to our lives today? These principles still apply in the twenty-first century workplace. These principles still govern the relationship between employers and employees.

Your view of the workplace

How you view your work can make a world of difference, not only in your life but in the lives of everyone around you. Some people view work as a necessary evil, a curse, an ordeal of drudgery that must be endured in order to put food on the table. These people hate their jobs, hate their bosses, and often become so embittered that it's difficult and unpleasant to be around them.

And let's face it, we can't all be thrilled with our jobs. Some people have jobs that take them to foreign capitals to interview presidents and kings, but most of us have to do much more mundane chores for a living. And I, for one, am grateful that there are people who do those chores and keep our society functioning.

If we are living Spirit-filled lives, we will see our work as a blessing, not a curse. We'll see our workplace as a mission field, an opportunity to impact others for Christ, a channel for witness and outreach to others. When we learn to see our work as Christ sees it, even a dysfunctional boss or a difficult coworker can become an evangelistic challenge and opportunity.

You may say, "But you don't know my boss! He's a slave driver!" But remember, Paul is addressing these words to people whose bosses *literally were* slave drivers.

Paul writes that we should render "service with a good will as to the Lord and not to man, knowing that whatever good anyone does, this he will receive back from the Lord, whether he is a bondservant or is free" (6:7-8). In other words, when we work, we are not working to please the boss in order to get a paycheck. We are working to please the Lord in order to win an eternal reward from him.

Do you have a difficult boss? An oppressive workplace? A job that seems pointless and discouraging? In those circumstances, you may feel like saying, "Why should I knock myself out for this job? My boss doesn't appreciate my hard work. I'm underpaid and overworked. Who needs this stress? I'm just going to take it easy and do the least I can get away with."

But God's Word reminds us who our real boss is. We serve the Lord. We work to please him, not men. As long as we think that we are working for an earthly boss, we will be miserable. But once we recognize that we work for God, even a miserable job becomes a ministry and a mission field. Jesus is our Master. He bought us when he died for us, and we became his willing slaves. He provides for us and watches over us, and he will reward us for the work we do here on earth. Even when all hell is breaking loose at the office, we can still sing praises to our real boss, our heavenly Master.

Even in the most stressful and unpleasant circumstances at work, we can call upon our heavenly Master and say, "Lord Jesus, Boss of the Universe, fill me with your Holy Spirit. Use me and help me to glorify you in this place. Strengthen me in this tough situation so that your light will shine in my life. Help me to present my faithfulness in this job as an offering and a sacrifice unto you, Lord."

When we are continuously filled with the Spirit, we will have the right perspective on our work. And when we have the right perspective, we will have the right attitude. And when we have the right attitude, we will be faithful on the job. And when we are faithful on the job, God will reward us in ways we never dreamed possible.

A word to bosses

Paul addresses not only slaves but slave masters. He talks not just to employees but to employers when he writes:

> Masters, do the same to them, and stop your threatening, knowing that he who is both their Master and yours is in heaven, and that there is no partiality with him (6:9).

Paul, inspired by the Holy Spirit, commanded employees to work diligently, as to the Lord. Now he also commands employers to treat their workers well, without threats or abuse. Why? Because God is the Master of both the slave and his master, of both the employee and the employer—and with God, there is no partiality. God sees the master and slave, employer and employee, as equals. He is not impressed with titles and positions. To God, the CEO in the corner office and the lowliest clerk in the mailroom are on an equal footing.

So bosses, as you exercise your earthly authority, make sure you do the will of the One who has authority over you. Obey God first and foremost. Please him. Be submissive to the authority of your heavenly Master.

This kind of admonition to slave-masters was unheard of in Rome at that time. A master's authority over his slaves was absolute, up to and including the power of life and death. Here, Paul imposes on slave-masters the same principle he commanded husbands and wives to obey: "submitting to one another out of reverence for Christ" (Ephesians 5:21).

Why does Paul introduce such a radical transformation in the relationship between master and slave, employer and employee? Because they both have the same heavenly Boss, the same Lord. Before God, they are both equal—and they are both accountable to him. They will both be rewarded by God, because he is the One who sees the very secrets of our hearts. This was a radical, revolutionary statement in Paul's day.

Paul makes a parallel statement in another letter: "Masters, treat your bondservants justly and fairly, knowing that you also have a Master in heaven" (Colossians 4:1). Justice and fairness for slaves was unheard of in that day.

But a godly employer is to reflect Christ to his employees. He is to be fair and just. He is to look out for their well-being. He is to care for their interests and protect them from harm. He is to respect them because respect for all people is honoring to God—and God does not play favorites.

All of God's children are equal in his sight. This is true whether you are a husband or wife, parent or child, master or slave, employer or employee. All of God's children deserve equal love, equal care, and equal justice. And we should all equally submit ourselves to our common Master.

Paul wrote a short New Testament letter to a man named Philemon, a Christian businessman and a slave-master. Philemon had a slave by the name of Onesimus, who had wronged Philemon, and then fled. In the Roman Empire, when a fugitive slave was captured, he was branded on the forehead so that he would always be known as an untrustworthy slave. This was likely the fate that awaited Onesimus if he were captured and returned to Philemon.

While Onesimus was on the run, he met the apostle Paul, and Paul led him to Christ. So Paul wrote to Philemon—a friend, a man he had known for years—and he asked him to receive Onesimus back "no longer as a bondservant but more than a bondservant, as a beloved brother" (Philemon 1:16a). Whenever the brotherhood of Spirit-filled believers is found, barriers are removed.

Your workplace, your mission field

Alfred Braca was a bond trader who worked for Cantor Fitzgerald, a financial services firm, on the 105th floor of one of the World Trade Center towers. He loved his family, his church, and his Lord. He was always telling others about the love of Jesus Christ. He gave generously to Christian missionaries and to Fellowship of Christian Athletes.

Around the office, some of his more jaded and worldly colleagues would sometimes make fun of him because of his devout and outspoken Christian beliefs. Their nickname for him was "The Rev."

But when people were going through a crisis, they would come to Al Braca and ask him to pray for them.

One such crisis was the 1993 bombing of the World Trade Center. Al and his coworkers had to evacuate, hurrying down seemingly endless flights of stairs to get to the ground level. As they went, his coworkers asked him, "Al, are you praying for us?" And Al replied, "I've got you covered."

On September 11, 2001, the World Trade Center was attacked again. This time, Al and his coworkers couldn't get out. But someone spoke with Al by cell phone after the plane hit the tower. Al couldn't talk long. He had gathered dozens of his colleagues around him, and he was sharing Christ with them and praying with them as the smoke billowed around them.

To Al Braca, working for Cantor Fitzgerald near the top of the World Trade Center was not just a job. It was his calling, his ministry, his mission field—and he gave his life doing what God had called him to do.

What has God called you to do? What is your ministry? Where is your mission field? Whatever job you do, work as to the Lord, not to men. If you offer your life and your career to the Lord and ask him to bless it, he will use you to change lives—and impact eternity.

13

Life Is a Battlefield

Ephesians 6:10-17

During World War II, the German forces under Field Marshal Erwin Rommel were beating the Allies in North Africa. Rommel was known as Desert Fox because he outfoxed the Allies for a long time. The fortunes of war changed when the Allies sent Field Marshal Bernard Montgomery to lead the Allied troops, defeating the Desert Fox in the Battle of El Alamein.

After the battle, Hitler recalled Rommel to Germany. Rommel told Hitler that the war was lost, and Germany should try to negotiate an honorable settlement with the Allies. Hitler agreed that the war was lost, but he refused to publicly acknowledge defeat. In fact, Hitler launched a propaganda offensive, claiming a German victory in North Africa. Had Hitler taken Rommel's advice and sued for peace, many thousands of lives would have been saved. But Hitler's arrogant pride would not allow it—and many soldiers and civilians were needlessly slaughtered as a result.

In many ways, the time between the defeat in the Battle of El

Alamein and the Allies' ultimate victory is like the time between the ascension of the Lord Jesus Christ and the time of his return. When Jesus rose from the dead, Satan was defeated. Through his death and resurrection, Jesus had rendered Satan powerless. But Satan, like Hitler, refuses to concede defeat. He refuses to accept his inevitable destruction.

So for a time, Satan continues stirring up trouble. He bellows his defiance. He attacks and destroys lives and refuses to surrender.

But soon—maybe sooner than we imagine—we will see Satan in chains. Soon we will see him in the lake of fire. Soon even Satan will bow before our victorious Lord Jesus. Until then, Satan will continue to wreak havoc in this world. He will try to lead God's children astray.

Though Satan has already lost the war, he continues to battle on.

On the attack

We now come to one of the most profoundly practical sections in Paul's letter—and, in fact, in all of Scripture. Paul writes:

> Finally, be strong in the Lord and in the strength of his might. Put on the whole armor of God, that you may be able to stand against the schemes of the devil. For we do not wrestle against flesh and blood, but against the rulers, against the authorities, against the cosmic powers over this present darkness, against the spiritual forces of evil in the heavenly places (6:10-12).

Some Christians ask, "Why do we have to fight Satan? Can't we just ignore him? Can't we just pretend that Satan doesn't exist?" That's exactly what the deceiver wants people to think—that he doesn't matter, that he doesn't exist, that he has no influence in the world, and we can simply ignore him.

A 2002 survey conducted by the respected Barna Research Group found that 55 percent of all Protestants and 75 percent of all Catholics in America do not believe in the existence of Satan. These Protestants and Catholics believe that Satan is a symbol of evil, not a real malevolent being.[17] This is nothing short of astounding. A majority of people who call themselves Christians do not believe what their own Bibles teach about the nature and origin of evil in the world.

Whether you like it or not, whether you accept it or not, if you are born of God, if Jesus is your Savior and Lord, then you are at war. You will be attacked. Although Satan is a defeated enemy, he refuses to lay down his arms and accept his defeat. In fact, he is on the attack every single day. And in those moments when he is not directly assaulting you, he is plotting his next move.

That's the bad news. Here's the good news. Those who are spiritually equipped for the battle will be victorious over Satan. Demonic powers fight dirty. Like terrorists, they look for weakness and vulnerability, and they attack without warning. There are no spiritual Geneva Conventions, no rules for fighting fair, and the forces of Satan wouldn't obey such rules if they existed. Satan and his fellow demons are utterly ruthless, cunning, and conceited.

The enemy of our souls seldom attacks in the open. He pretends to be an angel of light, deceiving us and lulling us into a false sense of security—then he strikes when we are defenseless. He is a wolf with a closet filled with sheep costumes. His wiles are endless. And he is probably the most crafty when he succeeds in convincing people that he does not exist.

The armor of God

When Jesus began his ministry and he was alone in the wilderness to be tested, Satan was there to attack him. And again, in the closing moments of the Lord's ministry, during his agony in the garden of Gethsemane, Satan was there to attack him. And every time Jesus was attacked by Satan, he defeated Satan through the power of the Word of God. It is only in the strength of our victorious Lord that we are able to withstand Satan's attacks.

And that is why Paul writes, "Be strong in the Lord and in the strength of his might." If you and I try to go to war with Satan in our own strength, our own wisdom and power, we will surely be defeated. That's why we need to put on the full armor of God, and we need to wear our armor 24/7. Paul reminds us that we do not fight against a mere flesh-and-blood enemy, nor are we struggling with minor spiritual opponents. Our enemies in the spiritual realm are rulers, they are authorities, they are the cosmic powers that control this present darkness. They are spiritual forces of evil in the heavenly places. That is why Paul goes on to write:

> Therefore take up the whole armor of God, that you may be able to withstand in the evil day, and having done all, to stand firm (6:13).

Why does Paul tell us to wear our spiritual battle armor? So that we may be able to stand. Many Christian soldiers have deserted the battlefield, they have given up the fight, they have ceased to stand. Many Christian soldiers have lost their spiritual nerve and their spiritual footing. They have fallen and have allowed Satan to walk all over them.

When a Christian soldier falls, he or she gives Satan an open doorway to walk into the church and into the family. Today, Satan has walked all over many families, many marriages, and many children. Satan is walking all over many Christian relationships, destroying churches and Christian testimonies. The spiritual battlefield is littered with the bodies of those who have fallen, who have not been able to stand in the crossfire of spiritual warfare. They did not wear their armor. They dropped their weapons. They ceased to be warriors for the cause of Christ.

Charles Templeton was one of these fallen warriors. Templeton was a writer, speaker, and newspaper cartoonist for *The Globe* of Toronto. One night in 1936, he prayed for God to reveal himself—and he felt "an ineffable warmth" come into him. Soon afterward, Templeton became a preacher and used his cartooning skills to illustrate chalk talks at youth rallies. Templeton became a close friend of Billy Graham, and along with Torrey Johnson, they cofounded Youth for Christ International in 1946. Templeton often toured with Dr. Graham, and they preached to enormous crowds and led untold thousands of people to Christ.

Templeton began to feel he needed a deeper understanding of theology, so he attended Princeton Theological Seminary in 1948. In the early 1950s, he began hosting a weekly religious TV show, *Look Up and Live*, on CBS. But while studying theology as well as agnostic works, such as Thomas Paine's *The Age of Reason*, Templeton went through a crisis of doubt. Evidently, he did not arm himself against satanic attacks. As he later recalled, "My mind was at war with my spirit." In reality, it was Satan himself who was at war with Charles Templeton's spirit—and Templeton's spirit was unarmed. In 1957, this man who had led many to Christ abruptly declared himself to be an agnostic.

In 1996, Christian journalist Lee Strobel interviewed eighty-year-old Charles Templeton in his Toronto apartment. Strobel asked him, "What is your opinion of Jesus at this stage of your life?"

Templeton's voice became "melancholy and reflective," Strobel recalled. Templeton replied that Jesus "was the greatest human being who has ever lived. He was a moral genius. His ethical sense was unique. He was the intrinsically wisest person that I've ever encountered in my life or in my reading."

"You sound like you really care about him," Strobel said.

"Well, yes. He's the most important thing in my life...I adore him...Everything good I know, everything decent I know, everything pure I know, I learned from Jesus." Then Templeton's voice quavered as he slowly said, "I...miss...him!" And Templeton began to weep.

Moments later, Templeton regained control of his emotions, brushed away tears, and waved his hand, adding, "Enough of that." Strobel wasn't sure if Templeton meant he wanted no more tears—or no more questions about Jesus.

Five years after that interview, Templeton died of complications related to Alzheimer's disease, and his old friend Billy Graham was one of the last people to visit him. Even though Charles Templeton missed Jesus and admired Jesus, he never claimed that he returned to faith in Jesus. Only God knows if he did.[18] But we do know that from the time he publicly turned away from the faith in 1957 until his death in 2001, Charles Templeton was like a corpse on the battlefield of spiritual warfare, felled by Satan, unable to stand.

Charles Templeton is not alone. Many who were once warriors for Christ, who had once served the Lord faithfully in the past, have been knocked down by Satan. They may have witnessed effectively, they might have even won many people to Christ, yet they ended up in a state of defeat, victims of Satan's spiritual attacks. They were defeated because they failed to put on the full armor of God.

The armor of God enables us to stand firm even in the face of a full-on, nuclear-strength satanic attack. The armor of God can enable us to stand—and to keep on standing. The greater the battle, the sweeter the victory. And the sweeter the victory, the greater the joy. If you want to experience victory over Satan, then discover the full armor of God and wear it into battle.

An inventory of your armor

The full armor of God consists of six items, which Paul describes in these verses:

> Stand therefore, having fastened on the belt of truth, and having put on the breastplate of righteousness, and, as

> shoes for your feet, having put on the readiness given by the gospel of peace. In all circumstances take up the shield of faith, with which you can extinguish all the flaming darts of the evil one; and take the helmet of salvation, and the sword of the Spirit, which is the word of God (6:14-17).

Let's look at each item of the full armor of God.

1. The belt of truth. The belt of truth uses the image of the wide leather belt that was wrapped around the soldier's waist. The soldier would tuck his tunic into the belt since wearing a free-flowing robe in the battlefield would be a hindrance to running and moving freely, and would cause the soldier to easily fall and stumble.

A Christian who does not encircle himself with the truth of God will fall for the devil's lies. Those who are indifferent to God's truth have left themselves wide open and vulnerable to the deceit of Satan.

2. The breastplate of righteousness. This plate of hardened armor protected the heart, lungs, and other vital organs of the soldier. The breastplate of righteousness protects the Christian in much the same way. The righteousness of Jesus Christ is reliable and sure. Jesus accomplished our salvation on the cross, and Satan can never take his righteousness away from us. Whenever the enemy assaults us with doubt about our salvation, or accusations about sins that God forgave and forgot long ago, we can say, "I am covered by the righteousness of the Lord Jesus Christ. His Word has promised, 'There is now no condemnation for those who are in Christ Jesus'" (Romans 8:1).

We also put on the breastplate of righteousness through our obedience to the Word of God. This means that we live in reliance on God's Spirit for the power to live in obedience to God's will. As Paul wrote in Ephesians 5:18, we continuously seek to "be filled with the Spirit" as we give him control of our lives, day by day, hour by hour, and moment by moment.

Unfortunately, many Christians have gotten a false impression of what it means to live in obedience to God's Word and God's will. Some believers have gotten the idea that obedience means being busy with church work—with rituals, activities, and programs—and many churches have encouraged this false idea. This amounts to handing out paper armor to the members of the church. Being busy in the church is not the same thing as obedience to God; it's not the same thing as the breastplate of righteousness. It's possible to be very busy at church while neglecting to live for Christ in the workplace and the neighborhood and the family.

Satan can pierce our paper armor of churchianity with ease. To protect ourselves in spiritual warfare, we must put on the bullet-proof, arrow-proof, dart-proof armor that is the breastplate of righteousness. If you go into battle without it, you are practically asking to be wounded and pierced by Satan's relentless attack.

3. The gospel boots. Paul writes, "as shoes for your feet, having put on the readiness given by the gospel of peace." The gospel of peace is the irrefutable truth that in Christ, and in him alone, we are now at peace with God and with one another. The believer who stands shod in the boots of the gospel is not afraid of the enemy. When we are attacked, we had better not be wearing flip-flops! Our feet need to be protected by the tough, reliable boots of the gospel of Jesus Christ.

4. The shield of faith. Roman soldiers generally used one of two kinds of shields. One was a small shield, about two feet in diameter, tied to the arm to protect a soldier in hand-to-hand combat. The other—the kind that Paul writes of here (we know this because he used the specific word for this type of shield)—is a full-body shield. It is about five feet high and two and a half feet wide, and designed to protect the soldier's entire body. Made of wood and covered with metal, this shield was capable of deflecting the enemy's pitch-soaked flaming arrows.

Paul writes, "In all circumstances take up the shield of faith, with which you can extinguish all the flaming darts of the evil one."

Flaming arrows are an apt picture of the temptation and doubt that Satan continually throws at us. If Satan can succeed in making us doubt God's love and care, or in making us question our own salvation, then his arrows will burn their way into our souls. Every time Satan is able to get us to distrust God, one of his arrows gets through. Sin begins when we believe Satan's lie and begin to doubt God's promises. The shield of faith protects us from Satan's flaming arrows.

5. The helmet of salvation. The helmet protects the brain, the seat of the human mind. One of Satan's most powerful attacks is in the area of the mind. If Satan can distort and twist our thinking, if he can convince us that our salvation is not assured, if he can get us to doubt God's Word or God's love for us, he will be able to lure us into sin. If he can discourage us and get us to view ourselves as failures in God's eyes, then he can prevent us from being effective servants of Christ.

So it is important that we remember at all times that we are saved by grace through faith, not through our own works. When we trust fully in the salvation Jesus purchased for us on the cross, we protect our minds from Satan's attack. The helmet of salvation is an essential piece of the full armor of God.

6. The sword of the Spirit, which is the Word of God. All the previous items of the soldier's armor are meant for defensive purposes. But the sword is both offensive and defensive. It is meant both to attack the enemy and to fend off the enemy's blows.

When we seek to lead people to Christ and rescue them from Satan's clutches, our best weapon is the sword of the Spirit, the Word of God. The Bible is authored by the Holy Spirit, the same Holy Spirit who indwells us and gives us power and the words to say. Christians who try to lead others to Christ by depending on human techniques will fail.

Ultimately, we don't convert anyone to Christ; the Spirit himself does the work of converting people, and he does so by using Christians who make themselves available as channels for his power. The more Scripture we know and can quote from memory, the more of God's own words the Spirit can call to our minds and speak through us.

God's Word is flawless and faultless. It is complete and authoritative. It is effective and decisive. God's Word is the source of all truth and all joy, all power and all spiritual maturity. The Word of God is a sword that slices through people's defenses. It pierces the conscience and awakens the spiritually dead.

Safe from attack

When I was a little boy, I ran away from home a number of times. My older siblings and my parents tried everything they could think of to stop me. We lived on the fourth floor of an apartment building. In the middle of the building was a big stairway, and it went down all four floors. One day when I was about four or five, I was up to my usual antics and decided to try to run away. As I took off down the stairs, I kept looking back and noticed that no one was following me. So instead of running down the stairs, I took my time.

What I didn't know was that my family wasn't following me because they were *already on the ground floor*, waiting for me at the bottom of the stairs. When I reached the ground floor and saw my family there, I was startled out of my wits. I turned and bounded up those four flights of stairs in practically no time flat!

Believers who run away from God, who try to escape obedience to his Word, think they're getting away with something. In reality, they are bringing pain and peril to themselves. They are leaving themselves defenseless. When Satan attacks them, he will show no mercy.

The further you run from God, the longer the trip home. Disobedience to the Word of God and rejecting the promises of God can produce nothing but a vicious attack from the enemy of our souls. Do not run away from God, my friend. Do not wander from his Word.

Imagine a little child walking hand in hand with Daddy. Suddenly, a vicious dog barks from the bushes nearby. Picture how quickly that child will climb into Daddy's arms. If the child is like I was, constantly running away, what will that child do when the dog barks—or worse, when the dog attacks? How long will it take for that child to run home? Will the child even make it home?

Don't take chances with your Christian walk. Take up the whole armor of God. Wear it all day, every day so that you may be able to withstand whatever Satan throws at you in the evil day. Wear it—and whatever comes your way, you will stand.

14

The Power of Prayer

Ephesians 6:18-24

As we come to the closing verses of Ephesians, it's not surprising that Paul concludes with the most important element of the Christian life. It's as if he is saying that, in order to experience victory over Satan, we must live in a state of continuous prayer.

In fact, prayer is the power behind each of the six pieces of equipment that make up the full armor of God. As in the words of the old hymn "Stand Up, Stand Up for Jesus," we must "put on the gospel armor, each piece put on with prayer." Putting on the whole armor of God is not a ritual we perform once and we are done. It is a lifestyle of total dependence and reliance on God, and the way we put on the full armor of God is through prayer.

Paul does not include prayer as a seventh piece of spiritual armor because prayer is so much more than just one piece of armor. Prayer is the act that seals our armor into a single protective unit. We fasten the belt of truth with prayer. We put on the breastplate of righteousness with prayer. We cinch up the boots of the gospel of peace with prayer. We strap on the shield of faith with prayer. We clamp the helmet of salvation to our heads with prayer. We wield the sword of the Spirit in an attitude of prayer.

Prayer is not one of the things we do. It's the main thing we do, the most basic and essential thing we do to prepare for spiritual battle. The act of prayer is our spiritual food and our spiritual drink. Prayer is the very air we breathe. We breathe out our praise and petitions and intercessory requests to God, and we breathe in the peace and comfort and assurance that his Spirit speaks to us in prayer.

I have never met anyone who said to me, "Michael, I breathed yesterday so I don't need air today," or "I ate yesterday so I'm not going to eat today," or "I had a drink of water yesterday so I don't need a drink of water today." Breathing, eating, and drinking meet the daily, ongoing needs of our bodies, and prayer meets the daily, ongoing needs of our soul and spirit.

Let's pay close attention, then, to what the apostle Paul says to us about prayer in the closing lines of Ephesians:

> praying at all times in the Spirit, with all prayer and supplication. To that end keep alert with all perseverance, making supplication for all the saints, and also for me, that words may be given to me in opening my mouth boldly to proclaim the mystery of the gospel, for which I am an ambassador in chains, that I may declare it boldly, as I ought to speak (6:18-20).

In Luke 18, Jesus instructed his disciples to pray always and to never lose heart, never give up. The Lord knew that we would easily become bored and tired and discouraged in prayer. He knew that as we faced our spiritual battles, we would either pray always and with perseverance—or we would become defeated. And that is Paul's message to us in these verses: "praying at all times in the Spirit… keep alert with all perseverance."

Most of us feel guilty whenever we think about our experience with prayer. We all know that prayer is important, prayer is vital—yet we feel our prayer life is woefully inadequate. We believe in the power of prayer, yet we don't pray as we ought to.

But God does not want us to feel defeated. He wants us to walk in victory, and a clear understanding of prayer is the key to victory in our Christian walk.

Praying at *all* times

As we saw at the beginning of Ephesians, one of the key themes of this letter is the vast treasure house of God's blessings. After listing the many blessings in our treasure house, Paul realizes the danger these blessings pose. You might ask, "How can God's blessings put us in danger?"

We are in far greater spiritual danger in times of blessing than in times of brokenness. Times of blessing bring the temptation of becoming self-satisfied, self-sufficient, spiritually complacent, and arrogant. So Paul—who began this epistle by lifting us to the highest heaven by taking us into God's treasure house of blessings—now drags us to our knees. Paul is deeply concerned for us, and he wants to make sure we don't become spiritually arrogant.

In Ephesians 6:18, Paul uses the word *all* four times. He writes, "praying at *all* times in the Spirit, with *all* prayer and supplication. To that end keep alert with *all* perseverance, making supplication for *all* the saints." Why does Paul stress the word *all*?

Paul knew that most Christians pray...at some times...for some things...for some length of time...for some of their fellow Christians. But Paul wants us to replace the word *some* with *all*.

He tells us that we should pray "in the Spirit." What does that mean? It means we must allow the Holy Spirit to pray for us and through us. It means we should pray what the Holy Spirit prays, that we should link our petitions to his, and that we should join our will with his. We saw earlier that to be filled with the Holy Spirit means that as we surrender to the Holy Spirit and give him control of our lives, he will pray in us and through us.

In the Old Testament, the people used to pray three times a day. Paul says in the New Testament that, because Jesus opened heaven for us, we can pray all the time. We can pray without ceasing. We can be conscious of the presence of God at every waking moment.

When you face temptation, you don't need to go anyplace to find God. He is right there. You don't need to wait until just the right time to pray. He will hear you whenever you call to him. You don't need to follow a ritual or burn incense or speak to him in Elizabethan English. Just open your heart and cry out in all sincerity, "Lord, help me!" And he will hear you.

When you experience a blessing from God and you want to thank him, the process is exactly the same. You don't need to stand on ceremony or make sure that certain conditions are just right. He's always there. He can always hear you. Just tell him whatever is on your heart. Stop right where you are and say, "Lord, thank you!"

When you face trouble or evil, say, "Lord, surround me with your protection and your righteousness!" When you are about to witness to someone about your faith in Christ, breathe a quick prayer, "Lord, put your words of good news in my mouth."

The more you are continually aware of God's presence, the more prayer becomes like breathing—in and out, in and out, listening to his Spirit, speaking back to him in prayer. You soon find that you are sharing every thought with him—your wishes, your plans, your problems, your joys, your sorrows, your worries, your dreams, again and again, moment by moment, throughout the day. We are not only to pray at special times (such as mealtime and bedtime), but all the time and on every occasion, with perseverance and persistence.

The concept of continual prayer is difficult for many Christians. We live in a fast-moving society, and we want our prayers to be just like our other communications—our text messages and tweets and Facebook posts. We want to be able to click "send" and receive God's reply in seconds.

If we are really patient, we might wait a little longer on God—a day, a week, maybe two. But if we don't get an answer from God right away, we tend to give up. Jesus said, "Watch and pray." He told us in Luke 18 about the widow who kept haranguing the unjust judge until he gave her justice. We don't know how long that widow persevered. We only know that Jesus teaches that we are to practice a similarly intense level of perseverance in our prayers to God.

Persevering in prayer

In Luke 11, the disciples found Jesus praying, and they asked him, "Lord, teach us to pray." So Jesus taught them the model of prayer we call the Lord's Prayer. But he didn't stop there. He went on to tell them a story about a man who knocked on his neighbor's door in the middle of the night to ask for bread. The man knocked and knocked and refused to give up until the friend got out of bed and gave him the three loaves of bread he wanted. Jesus also asked a series of questions:

> "What father among you, if his son asks for a fish, will instead of a fish give him a serpent; or if he asks for an egg, will give him a scorpion? If you then, who are evil, know how to give good gifts to your children, how much more will the heavenly Father give the Holy Spirit to those who ask him!" (Luke 11:11-13).

Notice that question: If you mere sinful human beings know how to give good gifts to your children, *how much more* will God, your heavenly Father, give good gifts, especially the gift of the Holy Spirit, to you?

The tragedy of the prayer life of most Christians is that we seem to become serious about prayer only when we face a crisis. If you are a mother or father, you can imagine how you'd feel if your children seldom called you, and the only time you heard from them is when they wanted something from you. "Mom! Dad! I have an emergency! Help me!" Or they only came to visit when they wanted money or some favor from you. How, then, do you think God feels about your prayer life?

Now, there's nothing wrong with praying in times of crisis. There's nothing wrong with spreading our needs and wants and petitions before God. But his Word tells us that we should pray continually, not just in times of need or crisis. When we pray constantly in the Spirit and a crisis arises in our lives, prayer is not going to be a strange activity or a last resort. It will simply be a natural passage in a long and continuous relationship.

Priorities in prayer

In this passage, Paul not only teaches about prayer, but he also asks the believers to pray for him and his fellow workers—and he makes this request in the context of his teachings on spiritual warfare. Paul wants the believers to understand that the Christian life is a battle, and that the believers' most important preparation for spiritual warfare is prayer. When we pray continually for spiritual power and spiritual victory, when we pray continually for the advance of God's kingdom, when we pray continually that the lost would turn to Jesus for salvation, then we are truly engaged in the battle.

You and I are on the front lines of this spiritual battlefield. Those on the front lines must know how to pray at all times, with all prayer and supplication, with all perseverance, interceding for all the saints. Yes, we still pray for ourselves, our needs, our concerns, our problems. But our prayers should not begin and end with ourselves.

Notice that Paul sets an example for what our priorities should be in prayer. When we become passionate about praying continually for God's work and God's kingdom, then we will find we don't need to pray for ourselves as much as we once thought. When we are passionate about interceding for others and take joy in praying for others, we will be amazed at how God takes care of all our needs.

The opposite is true as well. When a Christian is concerned only with his or her problems and concentrates prayer only on personal needs, it's as if that person is digging a pit of self-centeredness. And the pit gets deeper and deeper every time he or she focuses on those personal needs. One of the purposes of prayer is to lift our eyes to God and to make us more conscious of the needs of others; God never intended prayer to make us more self-focused and self-centered.

Jesus put it this way: "But seek first the kingdom of God and his righteousness, and all these things will be added to you" (Matthew 6:33). In other words, when you pray on behalf of God's agenda, his kingdom, his righteousness, his work, and his people, your needs will be met. All the things you need in life will be added to your life.

Even secular psychologists have discovered that this is true. When a depressed or anxious person focuses inward on his or her feelings and needs, that person tends to become more depressed and anxious. But the person who focuses on serving others tends to experience relief from depression and anxiety.

A Jewish friend, a prominent doctor in Atlanta, once asked me to speak at a medical convention.

"What I know about medicine would fit on the back of a postage stamp," I said.

"That's not the issue. I want you to speak on the power of prayer," he said. "We have empirical evidence that the power of prayer is far greater than all of our medicine can explain."

"You know that if I talk about prayer, I'm going to talk about Jesus."

"I know. And we still want you to speak to our convention."

The secular world is seeing what many Christians have missed: praying for others opens the floodgates of heaven. God pours out blessings, grace, and mercy on those who intercede for others and for God's kingdom.

An ambassador in chains

Paul wants the believers to pray especially for him, for his ministry as a missionary, and for the advance of the gospel of Jesus Christ. He writes:

> and [pray] also for me, that words may be given to me in opening my mouth boldly to proclaim the mystery of the gospel, for which I am an ambassador in chains, that I may declare it boldly, as I ought to speak (6:19-20).

Paul asks prayer for himself—not that the chains would stop making his ankles swell, or that the pain in his back would be relieved, or that he'd get a decent night's sleep in prison. No, personal comfort wasn't an issue with Paul. He was focused on the advance of the gospel. He said, in effect, "Pray that I will speak boldly when I declare the good news—even when threatened with torture and death."

Paul also reminded the believers that he was an ambassador for Christ, "an ambassador in chains." He was (as he had previously reminded the believers) "a prisoner for Christ Jesus on behalf of you Gentiles."

If you read between the lines, you can tell that Paul knew fear in prison. He had already suffered much. As he once wrote to the believers in Corinth:

> Five times I received at the hands of the Jews the forty lashes less one. Three times I was beaten with rods. Once I was stoned. Three times I was shipwrecked; a night and a day I was adrift at sea; on frequent journeys, in danger from rivers, danger from robbers, danger from my own people,

> danger from Gentiles, danger in the city, danger in the wilderness, danger at sea, danger from false brothers; in toil and hardship, through many a sleepless night, in hunger and thirst, often without food, in cold and exposure. And, apart from other things, there is the daily pressure on me of my anxiety for all the churches. Who is weak, and I am not weak? Who is made to fall, and I am not indignant? (2 Corinthians 11:24-29).

Paul knew that more dangers and threats lay ahead. He was tired, cold, aching, lonely, and yes, in spite of his great faith and spiritual maturity, he was afraid. Who wouldn't be? So he probably felt tempted to soft-pedal the gospel and make his message more palatable to the Roman culture. Perhaps if he weren't quite so bold, he could escape the next beating or flogging—or beheading.

So Paul didn't pray for more comfort or for better conditions in prison. No, he prayed for boldness in preaching the gospel. He knew that if believers everywhere prayed for his spiritual needs, his physical needs would be met as well.

Love incorruptible

Paul closes his letter with some final words of greeting and benediction, and he introduces someone we know very little about:

> So that you also may know how I am and what I am doing, Tychicus the beloved brother and faithful minister in the Lord will tell you everything. I have sent him to you for this very purpose, that you may know how we are, and that he may encourage your hearts (6:21-22).

We know very little about Tychicus. Paul mentions him in the final greetings of Colossians, 2 Timothy, and Titus, and Luke mentions him in Acts 20:4. Here in Ephesians, Paul tells us a little bit about Tychicus, calling him a "beloved brother and faithful minister in the Lord." That is high praise from Paul. It tells us that Tychicus is a man of proven faith and trustworthy character, a genuine servant of Jesus Christ. That is a title we should all aspire to earn. Paul goes on to write:

> Peace be to the brothers, and love with faith, from God the Father and the Lord Jesus Christ. Grace be with all who love our Lord Jesus Christ with love incorruptible (6:23-24).

Notice the family language Paul uses here. We are not just members of the same religious organization. We are *brothers and sisters* in the family of faith. We are children of the same heavenly Father.

Paul began this letter with the words: "Grace to you and peace from God our Father and the Lord Jesus Christ" (Ephesians 1:1-2). He closes this letter with a similar blessing: "Peace be to the brothers...Grace be with all who love our Lord Jesus Christ with love incorruptible." Paul's great wish for the church was that it be blessed with grace and peace.

I believe the peace Paul wishes for the church is both peace from without and peace from within. Paul has experienced great persecution and conflict throughout his ministry, and he knows firsthand how painful it is to suffer opposition. He writes these words, after all, from a Roman prison cell. So he prays that the church would experience peace from without, a freedom from persecution and opposition.

But I think it's even more important to Paul that the church experience peace from within. As he wrote in Ephesians 4:

> I therefore, a prisoner for the Lord, urge you to walk in a manner worthy of the calling to which you have been called, with all humility and gentleness, with patience, bearing with one another in love, eager to maintain the unity of the Spirit in the bond of peace. There is one body and

> one Spirit—just as you were called to the one hope that belongs to your call—one Lord, one faith, one baptism, one God and Father of all, who is over all and through all and in all (4:1-6).

If we love the Lord, we will love the body of Christ, the church, and we will be eager to maintain the unity of the Spirit in the bond of peace. We will love one another and serve one another. That, I believe, is the love Paul speaks of when he writes, "Grace be with all who love our Lord Jesus Christ *with love incorruptible*." An incorruptible love will seek to maintain the unity of the Lord's body in the bond of peace.

The church in Paul's day was under intense attack from Satan, from the Jewish religious leaders, and from the pagan Roman government. The world was at war with Christ and his church in the first century, and the world is still at war with us today in the twenty-first century. We live in a post-Christian world, and we need boldness to declare the gospel to the people in our neighborhoods and schools and workplaces. We need God's peace and grace and power so that we can spread the incorruptible love of Jesus Christ to everyone we meet.

So Paul's closing benediction in Ephesians is our benediction as well: "Peace be to the brothers, and love with faith, from God the Father and the Lord Jesus Christ. Grace be with all who love our Lord Jesus Christ with love incorruptible."

Notes

1. C.S. Lewis, *The Complete C.S. Lewis Signature Classics* (New York: HarperOne, 2007), 112.
2. John Wesley, "John Wesley Quotes," Gospel.com, http://www.gospel.com/bookmarks/John-Wesley-Quotes/2590.
3. MSNBC.com staff, "Christians Raise $400 to Help Ailing Atheist Who Railed against Their Nativity," MSNBC.com, March 22, 2012, http://usnews.msnbc.msn.com/_news/2012/03/22/10819081-christians-raise-400-to-help-ailing-atheist-who-railed-against-their-nativity; Billy Hallowell, "Christians Raise Funds to Help Atheist Who Threatened to Sue over TX Nativity Scene," TheBlaze.com, March 23, 2012, http://www.theblaze.com/stories/christians-raise-funds-to-help-atheist-who-threatened-to-sue-over-tx-nativity-scene/.
4. Department of Health and Human Services, "Youth and Alcohol: A National Survey," HHS.gov, June 21, 2002, http://oig.hhs.gov/oei/reports/oei-09-91-00652.pdf.
5. National Institutes of Health, "Teacher's Guide: Information about Alcohol," NIH Curriculum Supplement Series—Grades 7-8, http://science.education.nih.gov/supplements/nih3/alcohol/guide/info-alcohol.htm.
6. Reuters, "Excessive Alcohol Consumption Costs U.S. Economy Over $200 Billion Per Year," *Huffington Post*, October 18, 2011, http://www.huffingtonpost.com/2011/10/18/excessive-alcohol-consumption-us-economy-billion_n_1017223.html.
7. MADD, "Statistics," MADD.org, http://www.madd.org/statistics/.
8. From *Bits and Pieces*, May 1990, cited in "Alcohol," SermonIllustrations.com, http://www.sermonillustrations.com/a-z/a/alcohol.htm.
9. William R. Beer, *Strangers in the House: The World of Stepsiblings and Half-Siblings* (New Brunswick, NJ: Transaction, 2011), 5.
10. Pat Williams, *The Warrior Within* (Ventura, CA: Regal Books, 2006), 33.

11. William Barclay, *The Letters to the Galatians and Ephesians* (Louisville, KY: Westminster John Knox Press, 2002), 196.
12. Ibid., 197.
13. Dan Kindlon and Michael Thompson, *Raising Cain: Protecting the Emotional Life of Boys* (New York: Ballantine, 2000), 103.
14. Christian History, "William Wilberforce: Antislavery Politician," ChristianityToday.com, August 8, 2008, http://www.christianitytoday.com/ch/131christians/activists/wilberforce.html.
15. B.A. Robinson, "What the Bible Says About Slavery," ReligiousTolerance.org, August 7, 2007, http://www.religioustolerance.org/sla_bibl.htm.
16. Howard Dodson, "Slavery in the Twenty-First Century," *UN Chronicle*, May 8, 2008, http://www.smfcdn.com/assets/pubs/un_chronicle.pdf; BBC, "Millions 'Forced into Slavery,'" BBC News, May 27, 2002, http://news.bbc.co.uk/2/hi/2010401.stm.
17. Barna Research Group, "Americans Draw Theological Beliefs from Diverse Points of View," Barna.org, October 8, 2002, http://www.barna.org/barna-update/article/5-barna-update/82-americans-draw-theological-beliefs-from-diverse-points-of-view.
18. Pat Williams, *How to Be Like Jesus: Lessons on Following in His Footsteps* (Deerfield Beach, FL: Health Communications, 2003), 18-21.

About Michael Youssef

Michael Youssef was born in Egypt and came to America in his late twenties in 1977. He received a master's degree in theology from Fuller Theological Seminary in California and a PhD in social anthropology from Emory University. Michael served for nearly ten years with the Haggai Institute, traveling around the world teaching courses in evangelism and church leadership to church leaders. He rose to the position of managing director at the age of thirty-one. The family settled in Atlanta, and in 1984, Michael became a United States citizen, fulfilling a dream he had held for many years.

Dr. Youssef founded The Church of the Apostles in 1987 with fewer than forty adults with the mission to "equip the saints and seek the lost." The church has since grown to a congregation of over three thousand. This church on a hill was the launching pad for Leading the Way, an international ministry whose radio and television programs are heard by millions at home and abroad.

For more on Michael Youssef, The Church of the Apostles, and Leading the Way, visit apostles.org and www.leadingtheway.org.

Leading the Way Through the Bible Commentary Series

About the Series: The Leading the Way Through the Bible commentary series will not only increase readers' Bible knowledge, but it will motivate readers to apply God's Word to the problems of our hurting world and to a deeper and more obedient walk with Jesus Christ. The writing is lively, informal, and packed with stories that illustrate the truth of God's Word. The Leading the Way series is a call to action—and a call to the exciting adventure of living for Christ.

Leading the Way Through Daniel

Daniel lived as an exile in a hostile country, yet when he committed himself in faith to serve his limitless God, he achieved the impossible. How did Daniel maintain his bold witness for God in spite of bullying and intimidation? How did he prepare himself for the tests and temptations of life?

Like Daniel, believers today live in a culture that is hostile to biblical values. It takes great courage and faith to live as followers of Christ in a post-Christian world characterized by moral depravity, injustice, idolatry, and more. In *Leading the Way through Daniel*, Michael Youssef passionately shows readers that the resources Daniel relied on are equally available to them.

Sound teaching, vibrant illustrations, and a brisk conversational style will enable readers to take the truths of the book of Daniel and apply them to the pressures, trials, and temptations they face in today's culture.

Leading the Way Through Joshua

The book of Joshua contains some of the most compelling and relevant truths for our lives today. It is the story of "trembling heroes"—people filled with fear who overcame those fears and accomplished the impossible through reliance on God.

In *Leading the Way through Joshua,* Michael Youssef translates the challenges Joshua and the nation of Israel faced into challenges that are familiar to everyone. God calls people to follow Him, to conquer the Jerichos in their lives, to stand against the idolatry in our land. God calls Christians to tell the world about His covenant love, expressed through the life, death, and resurrection of His Son, Jesus Christ.

Readers of this devotional commentary will discover how to turn the insights of Joshua into action in their own lives. It will motivate them to step up, to be strong and courageous, to obey God, and to go wherever God sends them.

Coming March 2013

Leading the Way Through Galatians

It's tempting for Christians to think they can experience God's life and power through church attendance, religious symbols and rituals, and good deeds. But as the book of Galatians makes clear, religion means nothing unless believers are connected to the *source* of God's life and power.

In *Leading the Way through Galatians,* Michael Youssef applies Paul's message to the churches in Galatia to the challenge of living as authentic Christians in the twenty-first century. The message of the Gospel is a message of freedom from the law, freedom from bondage to sin, freedom from fear, freedom from judgment, and freedom from the need to perform and please others.

Through stories and contemporary insights, the timeless truths of Galatians will take on a new and powerful meaning as today's readers learn to apply this liberating message to everyday life and everyday situations.

Coming March 2013